WITHDRAWN
NDSU

WORDS, WORDS, WORDS!

WORDS, WORDS, WORDS!

BY

ERIC PARTRIDGE

BOOKS FOR LIBRARIES PRESS
FREEPORT, NEW YORK

First Published 1933

Reprinted 1970 by arrangement with Eric Partridge

PE
1585
P3
1970

STANDARD BOOK NUMBER:
8369-5365-7

LIBRARY OF CONGRESS CATALOG CARD NUMBER:
70-117912

PRINTED IN THE UNITED STATES OF AMERICA

FOR
MARY AND FRANCES LONG
WHO, IN THEIR MANY KINDNESSES,
WASTE NO WORDS AND YET
ACHIEVE ELOQUENCE

PREFACE

ALL these essays were written in 1931-2 except for three very short ones belonging to late 1930 and 'Euphemism' and '*Bloody*' written this year. Excepting four of the six longest, they have appeared in 'The Quarterly Review', 'The London Quarterly Review', 'The New Statesman', 'The Week-End Review', 'Action', 'John o' London's Weekly', and 'Everyman': I thank the respective editors for their kind permission to reprint. But every essay or study has been carefully revised, while many have been either amplified during revision or restored to their right proportions.

Several of the primrose paths here entered have been traversed as the result of temptation incurred in my preliminary researches for 'A Dictionary of Cant in the English Tongue', which I hope to have ready at the end of next year; but since this work embraces not only British but British Colonial as well as American criminal and tramp slang, the hope should perhaps be regarded as pious rather than prudent.

June 1933   ERIC PARTRIDGE

CONTENTS

	PAGE
PREFACE	vii

I. AN ETYMOLOGICAL MEDLEY

OFFENSIVE NATIONALITY 3
  Written, June 1932; published in 'John o' London', 1932

FOOTPADS AND HIGHWAYMEN 10
  Written and published in March 1931, in 'Everyman'

THE DEVIL AND HIS NICKNAMES 16
  Written, January 1931; published in 'John o' London', July 1931

FAMILIAR TERMS OF ADDRESS 23
  Written, September 1931; published in 'Action', October 1931

RHYMING SLANG, BACK SLANG, AND OTHER ODDITIES . 30
  Written, January 1931; published in 'Everyman', February 1931

THE ART OF LIGHTENING WORK 42

THE PHILOLOGY OF CHRISTMAS 53
  Written, November 1930; published in 'The Week-End Review', December 1931

ALL FOOLS' DAY 60
  Written, February 1931; published in 'The New Statesman', March 1931

REPRESENTATIVE NAMES 66
  Written, June 1932; published in 'John o' London', March 1933

AMERICAN CANT 72
  Written and published in 'The New Statesman', January 1931

WORDS, WORDS, WORDS!

	PAGE
THE WORD BLOODY	79
EUPHEMISM AND EUPHEMISMS	91

II. SEMI-BIOGRAPHICAL

ONE OF JOHN WESLEY'S SIDE-LINES 105
    Written, May 1932; published, October 1932, in 'The London Quarterly Review'

JOHNSON'S DICTIONARY 113
    Written, March 1931; published in 'Everyman', April 1931

A FALSTAFF AMONG ANTIQUARIES 122
    Written and published in 'Everyman', January 1931

III. ASPECTS OF SOLDIERS' SLANG: 1914–18

BRITISH SOLDIERS' SLANG WITH A PAST 135
    Written, January 1931; published in 'The Quarterly Review', April 1931

GERMAN ARMY SLANG 154
    Written, August 1931; published in 'The New Statesman', April 1932

THE SLANG OF THE *POILU* 162
    Written, June 1931; published in 'The Quarterly Review', April 1932

SOLDIERS' SLANG OF THREE NATIONS 181

APPENDICES

I BOXING DAY 209
    Written, 1930; published in 'Everyman', December 1930

II SOME GROUPS OF 'TOMMY' WORDS . . . 211
    Written, February 1931; published in 'A Martial Medley', May 1931

III THE *POILU* ON HIMSELF AND OTHERS . . . 219
    Written, July 1931; published in 'John o' London', February 1932

INDEX 225

I
AN ETYMOLOGICAL MEDLEY

OFFENSIVE NATIONALITY [1]

WE have all heard nationalities used offensively in such phrases as *Dutch courage, French leave,* and *young Turk* and felt that it must be a crime to be a foreigner; not so many have noticed that *English, Scotch, Welsh,* and *Irish* are also so used, even among ourselves.

Early in the sixteenth century, *Greek* and *Turk* were employed in an offensive way; from about 1580 to about 1650, *Spanish* was the scapegoat; in the seventeenth century, *Dutch* was common as an insult; in the eighteenth and nineteenth centuries, *French* meant unpopularity, as, in a less general manner, did *English, Welsh, Scotch,* and *Irish*; and during the War, and for nearly ten years afterwards, *German* conveyed an adverse opinion.

There were reasons, of course! For every word and every usage of words there is a reason—if only one can find it. Let us take in turn the ten 'national insults' just mentioned as typical of all such epithets, for *Swiss, Russian, Italian, Portuguese,* and others not dealt with here are also used in the same insulting manner. *Greek* designated a cunning person, a cheat, a card-sharper, as early as 1528, the great Oxford

[1] Cf. Professor Weekley's very different (and much better) essay in his 'Words and Names', published four months after this essay was written.

English Dictionary's example being 'In carde playinge he is a goode greke'. In these senses, *Greek*, though nowadays rare, was much used during the next three centuries. The phrase *a Greek gift*, which implies treachery, has a rather different origin, the reference being to the wooden horse so helpful in effecting an entry into Troy and to one of the most famous of all Latin verses, '*Timeo Danaos et dona ferentes*'—'I fear the Greeks even (*or* especially) when they bring gifts.'

Turk (the name arose during the Third Crusade) became 'offensive' about the same time as *Greek* : the first written record of the former follows that of the latter within a decade. In a ballad of 1536, *Turks* signifies cruel men, tyrants, savages, and some thirty years later the word did duty for a human figure on which to practise shooting ; at the end of the sixteenth century it became a bugbear with which foolish nurses frightened children ; towards the end of the next century, *Turk*—as we learn from B.E.'s dictionary of 'thieves' slang '—described 'any cruel hard-hearted man', a usage recorded by Captain Francis Grose, wit, porter-drinker, and antiquary, in his Rabelaisian 'Classical Dictionary of the Vulgar Tongue' (1785) and prevalent until the present day. Late in the nineteenth century, *young Turk* became popular to designate a mischievous child ; in 1904 a certain magistrate said to a very youthful offender : 'You are a young Turk, and a bad Turk, too ; I think I ought to send you to a reformatory school.' Turks, ever since the Crusades, have had a bad reputation, though it is pleasant to remark that in 1915 the British troops on Gallipoli found them to be brave and fair-minded soldiers.

OFFENSIVE NATIONALITY

The rivalry with Spain that became acute in the reign of Elizabeth soon had a result in language: in 1584 we note *Spanish* used unfavourably in the phrase, *Spanish practice*, deceitful or treacherous action. A survival was *Spanish coin*, which in eighteenth-century slang denoted 'fair words, and compliments', as we learn from Captain Grose, who records also the colloquial *Spanish trumpet*, 'an ass when braying', this being a good pun: an ass is a donkey, *don* a Spanish title; hence, *Don Key*. A still later survival is the nineteenth-century sailors' *Spanish navigator*, which Frank C. Bowen in his valuable and interesting little book, 'Sea Slang', defines as 'a term usually used in American ships for a foolish seaman whose only asset is his strength'.

Sailors likewise use *Dutch* in many unpleasant ways, a malpractice due to the tremendous trade rivalry between Holland and England in the seventeenth century, a rivalry that, though lessening, has continued. From the delightful Mr. Bowen we quote the following terms, used in the nineteenth century, but—some of them at least—originating in the seventeenth and eighteenth centuries: *The Dutch Brig*, 'cells on board ship or in the naval prisons'; *Dutch reckoning*, 'a faulty reckoning of position or distance run'; *Dutchman's anchor*, 'anything left at home, from the Dutch skipper who explained after the wreck that he had a very good anchor but had left it at home'; *Dutchman's breeches* (very wide and full), 'a small patch of blue sky'; *Dutchman's cape* (sometimes called *Cape Flyaway*), 'imaginary land seen on the horizon'. Sailors used the phrase *Double Dutch coiled against the sun* in the same way that we employ *Double Dutch*

6   WORDS, WORDS, WORDS !

when we mean unintelligible, gibberish, nonsense, a
usage that dates from the sixteenth century : in 1547
one Andrew Boorde remarked that ' In Denmark . . .
theyr speche is douche ', an example that I take from
Professor Ernest Weekley's most fascinating ' Etymological Dictionary of Modern English ', though rather
more of my examples necessarily come from the Oxford
English Dictionary. The irrepressible Grose gives
four *Dutch* phrases : *Dutch comfort*, ' thank God it is
no worse ', which, later, became *Dutch consolation* ;
Dutch concert, ' where everyone plays or sings a different
tune ', which, later, was often changed to *Dutch
medley* ; *Dutch feast*, ' where the entertainer gets drunk
before his guests ', with which compare the later *Dutch
treat*, everyone ' paying his own whack ' ; and *Dutch
reckoning*. Two other phrases call for mention : *The
Dutch have taken Holland*, an earlier form of *Queen Anne
is dead* ; and *Dutch courage*, or courage excited by
drink, to which in 1665 the poet Waller alludes in the
couplet :

> The Dutch their wine and all their brandy lose,
> Disarmed of that by which their courage grows.

French became ' offensive ' towards the end of the
sixteenth century (Ben Jonson in 1597 using *Frenchified*
contemptuously), but not at all general until near the
end of the seventeenth, for the grandeur of Louis XIV,
le Roi-Soleil, stank in the nostrils of all good Englishmen ; the chief eighteenth-century national offensive
epithet was therefore *French*, which remained so until
late in the nineteenth century. As examples we may
cite the following nineteenth-century terms : *French
pigeon*, a pheasant shot by mistake in the partridge

OFFENSIVE NATIONALITY

season ; *French prints*, indecent pictures—this we owe to Thackeray. In many British dialects, *French* still means new or foreign, *Frenchy* a foreigner ; and in old East Anglia *French* signified very bad, or in great trouble. *To take French leave* is not altogether ' offensive ', for, recorded first in Smollett, it refers to the eighteenth-century custom of departing from a reception or an at-home without bidding good-bye to one's host or hostess ; the French, by the way, have given us tit for tat by applying *filer à l'anglaise* (to go off in the English fashion) to an unheralded departure.

German was rarely used unpleasantly before the Great War. Early examples, however, are *German Duck*, which Captain Grose defines as ' half a sheep's head boiled with onions ', a name given—probably—because this was a favourite dish of the German bakers in London ; the plural has, in Yorkshire, long meant bugs, especially bed-bugs. *German* is also applied to things not genuine, as *German measles*, dating from just after the Franco-German War, and *German silver*. The War made German a very unpopular word ; in 1915 an indignant defendant in the Middlesex Police Court excused himself by saying that ' he called me a German and other filthy names '. Sometimes *Hun* and *Hunnish* were used instead. That folly, however, died out some five years ago.

Now we come to Great Britain and Ireland. *English* is the rarest of all the ' nasty nationalities ' considered in this article : it is used in only two connexions, *English burgundy*, which, meaning porter, is recorded by Grose in 1785, while seventy years later it bore the same meaning in the United States, where it has degenerated into thieves' slang ; and *English*

Malady or *English Melancholy* (that typically English complaint, the 'spleen'), these terms being seldom employed later than the year 1800.

Welsh, with its earlier form *Welch*, is so much more prolific that I can give only a few instances here. *Welsher*, a betting sharper, and *welsh*, to swindle out of money laid as a bet, are comparatively modern, there being no record of either before 1857, when ' The Morning Chronicle ' spoke of a man who ' got his living by " welching " and taking in the " flats " ' (*flats*, the opposite to *sharps*, *sharpers*, is a musical pun that has become part and parcel of colloquial English), while the respectable Miss Braddon, a best-seller of the mid-Victorian period, could use *welsher* in a transferred sense six years later and expect to be understood by her no less respectable public. It is not absolutely certain that *to welsh* and *welsher* are connected with Wales, but probability is all for the connexion. The very old nursery rhyme, ' Taffy is a Welshman, Taffy is a thief', may be responsible. *Welsh* is also a synonym for *Greek* and *double Dutch* as meaning unintelligible speech ; spelt *Welch*, it occurs in this sense as early as the year of Charles the First's death. Captain Grose gives *Welch comb*, ' the thumb and four fingers ' ; *Welch fiddle*, ' the itch ', as indeed is *Scotch fiddle* ; *Welch mile*, '. . . His story is like a Welch mile, long and tedious.' He records *Welch rabbit*, ' bread and cheese toasted ', but is wrong when he adds ' i.e. a Welch rare bit '. *Welsh rabbit* is correct : compare *Scotch rabbit* for the same thing, and *Bombay Duck*, meaning fish, the term representing a sailors' joke on the Mahratti word *bombila*.

The inimitable Grose is no less informative on *Scotch*

(*Scottish*, by the way, is more literary). He cites *Scotch bait*, ' a halt and a resting on a stick, as practised by pedlars ' ; *Scotch chocolate*, ' brimstone and milk ' ; *Scotch mist*, ' a sober soaking rain : a Scotch mist will wet an Englishman to the skin ' ; *Scotch warming-pan*, which had better remain undefined ; and *Scotch fiddle*, already noticed. Several other phrases—there are many !—that call for mention are *Scotch casement*, the pillory ; *Scotch coffee*, hot water flavoured with burnt biscuit ; *Scotch greys*, lice ; *Scotch prize*, a capture made by mistake ; *answer Scotch fashion*, to reply to one question with another, a conversational method with New Testament authority.

And last, but very far from least, is *Irish*. Both *Irish* itself and the colloquial *Paddy* are used for anger ; but *to get up one's Dutch* likewise means to become angry, as, in America, does *get one's Indian up*. In America, where almost every policeman and many politicians are Irish, the notice *No Irish need apply* hints ' You're not wanted here '. Remembering such phrases as ' talk double Dutch ' and ' that's Greek *or* Welsh to me ', we come with interest on *You're Irish*, you're talking gibberish. *Irish* has been a derogatory term since about 1650, though a certain type of beggar was called *Irish toyle* ninety years earlier. Grose in 1785 records *Irish beauty*, ' a woman with two black eyes ' ; *Irish evidence*, ' a false witness ' ; *the Irish arms*, thick legs ; *Irish apricots*, potatoes. Before closing the offensive, we may note that *Irishman's dinner* is a fast, *Irishman's hurricane* a dead calm, *Irishman's harvest* the orange season, and *Irishman's fire* one that burns only at the top.

FOOTPADS AND HIGHWAYMEN

FOOTPADS have not attracted very much attention; highwaymen are much more famous and their lives and exploits have been adequately treated. The best book on highwaymen is Captain Alexander Smith's ' General History of Highwaymen ', published early in the eighteenth century and brilliantly edited by Mr. Arthur Hayward a few years ago. The heyday of highwaymen was the period 1650–1710, but they continued to flourish until the end of the eighteenth century. Writing in October 1774, Horace Walpole, that most entertaining of all English letter-writers, complains that ' Our roads are so infested by highwaymen, that it is dangerous stirring out almost by day. Lady Hertford was attacked on Hounslow Heath at three in the afternoon. Dr. Eliot was shot at three days ago, without being resisted ; and the day before yesterday, we were near losing our Prime Minister, Lord North ; the robbers shot at the postillion, and wounded the latter. In short, all the freebooters that are not in India have taken to the highway. The Ladies of the Bedchamber dare not go to the Queen at Kew in an evening. The lane between me and the Thames is the only safe road I know at present, for it is up to the middle of the horses in water.' And it is of the period about 1770 that the best of all highwaymen stories has been written :

Mrs. Gaskell's ' The Squire's Story ', which is also one of the finest of any kind in the language.

A highwayman, obviously, had a horse. A footpad had no horse ; he was much lower than the mounted man in the hierarchy of rogues. The Oxford Dictionary defines a footpad as ' a highwayman who robs on foot ' and notes ' to footpad ', meaning to practise this art, and ' footpaddery ', the occupation of a footpad.

The various ordinary and the various slang words and phrases connected with footpadding or footpaddery throw some light on the class of men that descended to this method of gaining a livelihood. ' Footpad ' itself comes from cant, the ' secret ' language of thieves and other criminals as well as of vagrants (including gipsies), and it appears first in good English in the phrase ' though they assault us like footpads in the dark ', which occurs in 1673 in a play by Dryden ; the verb ' to footpad ' arrived in 1735 : ' footpad(de)ry ' not until late in the nineteenth century, as I gather from the Oxford Dictionary.

An undoubtedly earlier form is ' pad ', though it seems to have meant, at first, either a footpad or a highwayman. ' Pad ' originally was cant for a path or track, then for a road, and as early as 1567 we find that ' the high pad ' is the highway. Now ' pad ' for footpad does not derive direct from ' pad ', a road ; the road gave the word ' padder ', which meant a footpad, as we see from Rowland's entertaining book on malefactors : ' Martin Mark-all ', 1610 ; there we read that ' Such as robbe on horse-backe were called high lawyers and those who robbed on foot he called

Padders'. 'Padder' was soon abbreviated to 'pad', and as the original word was sometimes used loosely to mean also a highwayman or a robber, so 'pad' was also used in this way by careless writers. As early as 1638 the verb 'pad' meant to rob on the highway, to be a footpad, and a generation later 'padding' denoted either the profession or the practice of highway robbery. In the eighteenth century, one often distinguished between the mounted and the unmounted men by calling them, not 'highwaymen' and 'footpads' but 'high pads' and 'low pads'; and late in the century Captain Grose indicated that the general phrase for the activity of either class was 'to go out upon the pad', for, in cant and colloquialism, 'pad' could still mean the highway. Grose has two other interesting terms that might apply to either. 'Catching Harvest' signified 'a dangerous time for a robbery, when many persons are on the road, on account of a horse-race, fair, or some other public meeting'; on this point Defoe's 'Moll Flanders' offers a pertinent comment. Both highwaymen and footpads had assistants—for a consideration: these 'cruisers' were 'beggars, or highway spies, who traverse the road, to give intelligence of a booty'.

A word that came into use about the time of Grose's death in 1791 was 'toby', on which I find a brief and pregnant passage in John Camden Hotten's 'Slang Dictionary': 'TOBY. The road. The highwayman or swell robber was in the old days said to be " on the high toby ", from the high or main road, while those meaner fellows, the footpad and the cutpurse, were but " low toby men " from their frequenting the by-ways.' Sir James Murray, whose researches led to

FOOTPADS AND HIGHWAYMEN

such fruitful results, says that 'toby' is from Shelta, the cant spoken by Irish tinkers; but *tober* is also Romany, the language of the English gipsies, as we see from that fascinating book, 'No. 747; the Autobiography of a Gipsy'.

Highwaymen, indeed, had often been men of some social standing. As their activities are too well known to admit of description here, it will be more opportune to glance for a moment at some of the old names and relevant phrases. (Practically all these words are to be found in Grose's 'Classical Dictionary of the Vulgar Tongue', third edition, 1796. The quotations are from the same source.) 'Bully Ruffians' are those highwaymen 'who attack passengers with oaths and imprecations'.

'Chosen Pells': 'Highwaymen who rob in pairs, in the streets and squares of London: to prevent being followed by the sound of their horses' shoes on the stones, they shoe them with leather.' 'Pell' indicates an early pronunciation of 'pal'; this word was originally confined to the English gipsies, who still use it to mean a brother, a friend, or an associate. (See 'No. 747' and Borrow's 'Romano Lavo-Lil'.)

'Collector': simply a highwayman. But 'a highwayman who throws away or hides anything with which he robbed, to prevent being known or detected, is, in the canting lingo, styled a Dinger', from 'ding', to knock down.

'Gentleman's Master': 'A highway robber, because he makes a gentleman obey his commands, i.e. stand and deliver.'

Fancy names for a highwayman were, and are:

'Knight' or 'Gentleman of the Road', and 'Knight' or 'Gentleman' or 'Squire of the Pad'. Such refinements are analogous to 'Knight of the Shears' or 'Needle' or 'Thimble' for a tailor, 'Knight of the Rainbow' for a footman.

Somewhat akin is 'Land Pirates', which is a term borrowed from Shakespeare. Quite respectable as a description. But cant gives us the even more vivid phrase, 'His means are two pops and a galloper', i.e. two pistols and a horse : a nice way of saying that he is a highwayman, who might well use 'pop' as a verb : 'I popped the cull' would mean 'I shot the man'.

In 1914–18 a favourite word for 'to purloin' was 'snaffle', which comes from thieves' slang of the seventeenth and eighteenth centuries ; in the latter century it was therefore only natural that a highwayman should be known as a 'Snaffler'.

'Rum Padders' were 'highwaymen well mounted and armed'. This pure-cant term shows that in the old days 'rum' meant 'excellent' and was the opposite of 'queer' (also cant), meaning 'bad' : yet to-day there is little to choose between 'a rum cove' and 'a queer cove'. This, however, is a story that must be told at some other time.

'Scamp', which in good English either signifies a ne'er-do-well or is an affectionate reproach, began as a synonym for a highwayman, and a 'Royal Scamp' denoted 'a highwayman who robs civilly', while a 'Royal Foot Scamp' is 'a footpad who behaves in like manner'. Grose gives an alternative definition of royal scamps : 'highwaymen who never rob any but very rich persons, and that without ill-treating them '. In an anonymous poem written about 1754, a highwayman says :

> ... I never robbed a poor man yet
> Nor ever made a tradesman fret,
> I served the poor and robbed the great,
> Which brought me to this wretched state.

From the same poem (the full text is given in my ' Pirates, Highwaymen and Adventurers ') it appears that ' scamp ' was sometimes lengthened to ' scampman ', which is related to ' the scamp ' as meaning ' the highway as a place on which to rob ' or ' highway robbery ' or ' the profession of a highwayman '.

THE DEVIL AND HIS NICKNAMES

ALTHOUGH a serious, this is not a dreadfully serious essay. To those who wish to study in detail the Biblical and philosophical considerations attaching to the Devil himself and to his names, I recommend the following books: 'An Enquiry into the Scripture Meaning of the Word Satan, and its synonymous terms, the Devil, the Adversary, and the Wicked One', an anonymous book probably written by a certain Rev. Mr. Barker, 1772, very dry indeed; 'The Devil', by J. Epps, 1842, an informative, but again a rather dry book; more important and much more interesting than either of these is 'The Autobiography of Satan', by John R. Beard, D.D., 1872, easily readable and well worth reading; 'Bibliotheca Diabolica', 1874, this being a list of books dealing with the Devil; the best of all books on the subject, 'A History of the Devil and the Idea of Evil', by the great French philosopher, Paul Carus, who appeared in an English translation in 1900; less satisfactory to the thinker but much more pleasantly readable by the man in the street is another work from France, 'The Devil', by Maurice Garçon and Jean Vinchon, who, in English dress, came before the English public in 1929.[1]

[1] Since this essay was written, there has been published Arturo Graf's witty book wherein the Devil is shown to have died in

THE DEVIL AND HIS NICKNAMES

The Devil is famous in literature, and either he or his Prime Minister appears as the hero, or as the truly central character, of such works as Marlowe's ' Doctor Faustus ', Milton's ' Paradise Lost ', Defoe's ' Political History of the Devil as well ancient as modern ', Goethe's ' Faust ', Lamb's comic—and comical—poem on the Devil.

He figures largely in proverbs, of which the best known is ' Tell the truth and shame the Devil ' ; but some of the others are more pointed : ' The Devil is good when he is pleased ' (compare ' When the Devil is sick, the Devil a saint would be ') ; ' Talk of the Devil, and he'll either come or send ' ; ' An idle brain is the Devil's workshop ' (which gave rise to ' Satan still finds work for idle hands to do ') ; ' He must have a long spoon that will sup with the Devil ' ; ' Heaven sends meat (i.e. food), but the Devil sends cooks '.

Before we come to the nicknames, it is just as well to glance for a moment at the chief among the more dignified names by which we refer to *his Satanic Majesty* (a jocular term, on the analogy *his Catholic Majesty*). Most general of all is *Devil* itself, from Latin *Diabolus*, which comes from a Greek verb meaning to throw across, hence to slander ; ' the slanderer *par excellence* ' is the original meaning of *the Devil* and it was for a long time confined to *the Arch Fiend*. Yet in quite early times *Devil* became confused with *Demon*, from the Greek *daimon*, which signifies either a divinity or a guardian spirit (or ' tutelary genius ' as the learned

---

the late 1880's. See also Professor Weekley's ' Mumbo-Jumbo ' in ' Words and Names ' (October 1932, John Murray).

call it) ; the more usual English sense, that of an evil spirit, comes from the Greek *daimonion*, a little or minor divinity, through the Latin *daemonium*, the form used in the Vulgate (i.e. the fourth-century Latin version of the Bible) for either a heathen god or an ' unclean spirit '. *Fiend*, common to the Teutonic languages, of which English is of course one, appears as early as Anglo-Saxon times for Satan, and the adjective *fiendish* is now stronger than *demonic* just as *demonic* has long been stronger than *devilish*. One of the dignified names is *the Adversary*, which happens to be the translation of the Hebrew *Satan*, an adversary in general, from the Hebrew verb *satan*, to plot against ; even in Hebrew, *Satan* was occasionally used to designate *the Enemy* or *the Enemy of Mankind* ; in the English Bible, from Tyndale's version, 1525-31, onwards, *Satan* is the stock word for the Devil. Related with *Enemy* and *Adversary* is *the Tempter*, from the Latin *temptare*, to test, put to the test, later to try to attract, to allure, to tempt in the modern sense, the word *Tempter* first occurring in written English in the fourteenth century, for example in Wyclif. *The Serpent* is Biblical and to some extent mystical. *The Wicked One* established itself in the sixteenth century, *the Evil One* (thanks largely to Milton) in the next century, with the Scottish variation *the Evil Man*. We need do no more than allude to such terms as *the Prince of Darkness*, terms that always, as in Marie Corelli's novel, ' The Sorrows of Satan ', connote in the users a tendency to dramatize or to romanticize. *Lucifer*, properly the Morning Star, is a Latin word often employed for Satan, especially for Satan prior to his banishment from Heaven ; it appears very early in English, and is dignified by its occurrence in Shakespeare and Milton. The early history of *Beelzebub* is obscure, but from the New Testament use of the word to designate ' the prince of demons ' it early became—it appears in Anglo-Saxon of the tenth century—one of the popular names of the Devil, as in Langland and Shakespeare but not in Milton.

Beelzebub has come down in the world and is now more properly considered a nickname. So has *Mahoun*, which in the thirteenth and fourteenth centuries rightly meant Mahomet ; in the medieval sacred plays, Mahoun was often ' a false god ' or a monster, and related is the use of the word to denote the Devil. In this last sense the word is dead, except in dialect, where, like the other four words in this paragraph, it is often linked with ' old ' : *Old* (or *auld*) *Hornie, Nick, Ruffian, Thief.* Hornie is Scottish—Robert Burns employs it very effectively—and obviously connected with the horns that, like the cloven hoof, were always present in medieval pictures of the Devil. *Ruffian*, which comparatively seldom has ' old ' conjoined, was, in the form *ruffin*, the name of a fiend ; in at least one manuscript of a medieval sacred play, *Ruffian* occurs for the Devil ; and in thieves' slang of the sixteenth to eighteenth centuries it is spelt both ways and means the Devil : ' to the Ruffian ! ' corresponded with ' (go) to the devil ! ' *Thief* is usually *Ill Thief, Old* or *Auld Thief*, or *Old* (*Auld*) *Ill Thief*, and is properly Scottish. *Nick* is likewise more usually *Old Nick* ; although *Nick* is probably the *Nick* that forms the usual abbreviation of *Nicholas*, the precise reason why *Nicholas* should be especially connected with the Devil still remains unknown ; the earliest recorded use is as *Old Nick*, about 1643, this person being invoked to 'stand up for' the Roundheads.

The next group of nicknames is that in which 'old' always precedes the noun. The full force of 'old' is seen at its very best in *the Old One*, for *one* by itself gives no clue. Now 'old' has many, many meanings, but the most frequent are 'aged', 'belonging to old times, or to ages long past', 'well-known' (as in 'that's an old story!'), and 'experienced', hence 'clever', hence 'cunning', hence 'evilly cunning', hence 'wicked'; it is these last two shades of meaning which determine the significance of the *Old Devil* group, though 'old' has, at the same time, some reference to the primeval character of the Devil. *Old Roger*, frequent in the eighteenth century, is now obsolete. Another early name was *Old Boots*, which persists in the phrase, 'It's raining like Old Boots!', i.e. like the Devil! *The old Dragon* began by being literary, as in Milton, but, like *the Serpent* (degenerating to *the old Serpent*), it came to mean the most deadly of all 'snakes in the grass'; similar is *the old Impostor*. Jocose or at any rate colloquial were *Old Harry*, as in 'He played old Harry with the furniture', but now it often indicates nothing stronger than 'much' or 'hard',—*the old Gentleman*, which is short for the alternative *the old Gentleman in black*,—*old Scratch*, as in Smollett in 1762, and possessing the variations *old Scrat(t)*, *old Scratchem*. Some of these nicknames survive in the rural and urban dialects of Great Britain: moreover the dialects offer further nicknames that, in some instances, are still occasionally heard in slang: *old Bendy*, a North Country term; *old Bogey*, as in that entertaining book dealing with the Midlands,

THE DEVIL AND HIS NICKNAMES

Bartram's ' People of Clopton ', 1897 ; *old Botheration,* from Devonshire ; *old Boy,* an Irishism ; *auld Carle,* North Scotland ; *old Chap,* fairly common, and *old Child,* rare ; *old Cloots,* as in Robert Burns ; *old Dad,* Yorkshire ; *old Fellow,* common ; *auld Hangie,* another of the nicknames popularized by Burns and probably connected with *hangman* ; *old Hooky,* North Country, from the verb *hook,* to angle for, to catch, the Devil angling for and often catching the souls of men ; *old Lad,* very frequent in dialect, and *old Man,* much less frequent ; *old Nicker* or *Nickie* or *Nickie Ben,* all variations on *old Nick* ; *old Sam,* Lincolnshire ; *old Saunders* and the more friendly and familiar *Sanners* or *Sanny,* obviously Scottish ; *old Smith,* Aberdeenshire, from *(black)smith* and not from the surname ; *old Smoke,* Surrey, hence often in London until recent years, and hence also the phrase ' like smoke ', for ' like old Smoke ! ', i.e. ' like the Devil ! ' ; *owd Sooty,* Lancashire, while *old Soss* belongs to the rival county, where ' an ill-favoured soss ' denotes an ugly, big, fat man.

The next and last division of the Devil's nicknames consists of those terms which, used independently of ' old ', are either colloquial or frankly slangy. *Skipper* is slang and derives from the sense of captain, but one very rarely hears it nowadays. *Black Spy* is cant, the specialized slang of thieves, other malefactors, and vagrants ; common in the eighteenth century, it is now obsolete. Everyone, however, knows *the dickens !* as an exclamation, though few would care to hazard a guess as to its origin. I remember that as a boy I thought of it as being derived from the name of the great novelist ; but the expression occurs in 1598 in Shakespeare's ' Merry Wives of Windsor ' : ' I can-

not tell what the dickens his name is.' Heywood in
1600 has the same phrase, likewise D'Urfey in 1676.
There is the variation *a dickens*, as in Congreve (1687).
Note also *the dickens take you!*, used by Urquhart in
1653 and recorded in a dictionary two years later;
to play the dickens occurs in Smollett in 1771; *to go to
the dickens* was apparently not introduced until the
latter half of last century. The suggestions that *dickens*
is a corruption of *Nick* or of *devilkin* are ingenious but
unsubstantiated. Most probably *dickens* was substituted for *Devil* as having the same initial letter. *Deuce*
was once explained as coming from *Dusius*, a demon
or devil among the ancient Gauls, or even as from
Deus (God), but as Professor Weekley points out,
'there can be no reasonable doubt that *the deuce!* is
a dicer's exclamation at making the lowest throw, two,
French *deux*. We still use *deuce* for the two in cards.'
Annoyance begot superstition, and superstition the
idea that the devil was behind it; *the deuce!* came
to be synonymous with *the devil!*; and finally *deuce*
became a synonym of devil, as in Swift and Thackeray.
In strict truth, however, neither *dickens* nor *deuce* is a
perfect example of a nickname.

FAMILIAR TERMS OF ADDRESS

IT is hardly the fashion for Court circles to address one another as *mate, chum, bo,* such terms, except during the War, being confined to the lower classes, if such there be. But almost everybody has read or heard or, if a man, been addressed by one or another of the following : *mate, pal, chum* (English) ; *bo* or *buddy* (American) ; *digger* or *cobber* (Australian). Words that mean so much more than the *comrade* and *brother* of internationalism. In fact *comrade* generally indicates that the speaker is envious of the other's position, *brother* that he intends to get some of his money : ' If a man call you " brother ", put your hand in your pocket—and keep it there.'

The English terms, naturally enough, are much the oldest, and of these *mate* is centuries the earliest. From either Dutch or Low German, the word at first implied a partaking and sharing of meat. The earliest mention is 1380, when it occurred in a verse romance in the sense of an associate or a companion ; in 1440 it is recorded in the invaluable ' Promptorium Parvulorum ', the Latin-English dictionary that, since 1840, has attracted two different learned editions ; in a chronicle of 1568 we hear that ' the Duke of Yorke and his mates were lodged within the city '. From that date onwards, the word is very general, but in the examples I have given it is not a term of address :

in the narrower sense, *mate* is recorded first in 1450 and until about 1600 it was restricted to sailors. In 1858 John Camden Hotten, the lexicographer of slang and the founder of the publishing house of Chatto & Windus, defined it as ' the term a coster or low person applies to a friend, partner, or companion ; " me and my mate . . ." is a common phrase with a low Londoner '. Just fifty years later, Dr. Henry Bradley remarked : ' now only in working-class use '. In frequent use now in address, but originally equivalent to a dockyard labourer, is *matey*, an elaboration to be found in Marryat a century ago and listed by Hotten in his ' Slang Dictionary '. *Mate* itself has had its ups-and-downs. At first dignified, it came, like *companion*, to be used contemptuously ; in short, it followed the vicissitudes of its synonym *fellow*. Again, like *companion*, but unlike *fellow*, it has rehabilitated itself, ' always a difficult feat for either a word or a person ', as Greenough and Kittredge sagely observe in ' Words and their Ways '. Always, however, as *fellow* did at first, *mate* has ' implied friendly association ' (Professor Weekley in his delightful ' Words Ancient and Modern '). At one time, *messmate* was a variant : ' a companion, a camerade ', Grose, 1785. In certain dialects, *mate* has long been a common way of greeting a stranger, and in 1914–18 *mate* and *chum* were, among English soldiers, the most frequent terms of address ; in 1914–18 *mate* was also a synonym for friend or comrade, while *be matey* implied ' be a sport, be friendly ! '

Both *pal* and *chum* became established in what, roughly, we call the Restoration period. Ultimately cognate with a Sanskrit word for brother, through the

Turkish Gipsy *pral, plal,* likewise a brother, *pal* comes from the English Gipsy *pal,* originally a brother but derivatively an associate, a mate, hence a friend ; it is in print first in 1681-2, in a diocesan record, but it was doubtless used in speech long before that. During the approximate period 1700-1820 the word was under a cloud, for, in the region of cant, it then connoted villainy : an accomplice. In Grose's ' Classical Dictionary of the Vulgar Tongue ', we find that *chosen pells* were highwaymen who robbed in pairs, especially in the streets of London ; *pell* was an alternative spelling and pronunciation. In Gipsy also the word had a pejorative meaning in certain contexts, for while, in the glossary of ' Romano Lavo-Lil ', *pal* is defined simply as brother and we learn that *pal of the bor* is a hedgehog (literally, brother of the hedge), and while the English Gipsies say *pal* and *pen,* brother, sister, when they address one another, George Borrow remarks on the other hand, that *blowen* signifies ' a sister in debauchery as *pal* denotes a brother in villainy '. As late as Hotten the word bore the gloss, ' a partner, acquaintance, friend, an accomplice '. It was not until about 1890 that *pal* became respectable. Although it has never been current in dialect, it was common among soldiers during the War to designate a friend or a comrade, but it was rarely used in the vocative except with *old.* Men from Liverpool and Manchester will recall that the four ' city ' battalions of those parts were known as *the Pals,* and men from any part will remember that as *matey* connoted a specific act of friendliness, *pally* connoted a temperamental tendency to be companionable or ' chummy '.

Chum attains print for the first time in 1684, when

Creech, in his translation of Theocritus, dedicates one of the Idylls 'To my chum Mr. Hody of Wadham College'. In 1690 it appears in B.E.'s dictionary of cant. Sir James Murray's pronouncement (1905) that it is ' now chiefly in familiar colloquial use with schoolboys, fellow-students; also with criminals, convicts, &c.', is illuminating when set against Creech and B.E., and piquant when juxtaposed with Dr. Johnson's ' a chamber-fellow, a term used in the universities ', and Captain Grose's ' a chamber-fellow, particularly at the universities and in prisons '. Although, as the ' Oxford Dictionary ' says, the derivation of *chum* by abbreviation from *chamber* in *chamber-fellow*, *chamber-mate*, is unproven, this derivation, as Professor Weekley maintains in his ' Etymological Dictionary of Modern English ', is probably correct, for ' this was the age of clipped words (*mob*, *cit*, *bam*, &c.) '. By 1860 the word was ' recognized ' as meaning an intimate acquaintance. As friend or comrade it was more popular among non-Cockney troops in 1914–18 than either *mate* or *pal*, and it was very frequent indeed as a term of address. (Australians and New Zealanders, in addressing a Tommy, nearly always said *chum*, generally in the Lancashire form, *choom* : apparently the word amused them vastly.) Yet it is not a widespread dialect word. We may however note the pretty Essex custom, not quite obsolete, of calling one's wife *chum* or *oad chum*.

Wholly dialectal is *sorry* or *surry*, which was often heard among Yorkshire and Lancashire troops : ' Give us a light, sorry ! ', ' Eh, sorry, where are you going ? ' The word, in various forms, occurs in Irish and in many Northern and Midland dialects. Definitely a

FAMILIAR TERMS OF ADDRESS 27

corruption of *sirrah* and rarely anything but a vocative. In 1903 the late Joseph Wright, who, greatest of all dialect-lexicographers, was wont to call all his male students (even if aged thirty or more) *lad* and all his girl students *lass*, glossed the word thus : ' A term of contempt or familiarity, especially used to an animal or to a young person of either sex, or by boys among themselves.' But while familiar in tone in War and post-War days, contempt and undue familiarity cannot, after 1914, be laid at its door.

Even among English troops, *digger* came, in 1918, to replace to some extent the typically English vocatives *mate, pal, chum*, and *sorry*. This was due to the influence of ' the Diggers ', the Australian and the New Zealand troops, the former of whom never employed any vocative other than *digger* or *cobber*, the latter than *digger* : that is, among themselves. It is rarely that I can take exception to the comments in Fraser and Gibbons' valuable ' Soldier and Sailor Words and Phrases ', but here I must be contradictory and assert that *digger*, though more general, never displaced *cobber* among the Australians. *Digger* dates from the old gold-rush days, but it has not reached the ' Oxford Dictionary ' ; it is, of course, related to *diggings*, in university slang *digs*, for lodgings, apartment, or house, recorded since 1838. But *digger*, except as a term of address, has never been a synonym of *mate, pal, chum*, for friend or comrade or companion.

Cobber is much more obscure. In the ordinary way it means a friend, a comrade, and it is used freely in the vocative. It is an Australianism of thirty or forty years' standing, but is absent from the dictionaries of Murray, Wright, and Weekley, as from the dictionaries of slang, and even from Morris's 'Austral English' (1898). There are, however, two possibilities, both offered by Wright's 'English Dialect Dictionary'. In Cornish, there is *cobba*, a bungler or a simpleton: this may have migrated to Australia and there, as so often happens with emigrants, have been gradually altered. The other possibility is more likely: that *cobber* has developed from the Suffolk word *cob*, to form a friendship for, to take a liking to. But these theories must, I think, be discarded in favour of the fact that both Yiddish and pure Hebrew have the word *chaber*, a comrade, for Australian slang contains a number of Hebrew and some few Yiddish words, for instance *cliner*, *clinah*, a sweetheart.

No less picturesque are the two American vocatives, *bo* and *buddy*. *Bo* is an abbreviation of *hobo*, a late nineteenth-century Americanism of obscure origin. Most dictionaries define *hobo* as a tramp or a professional tramp, but properly a *hobo* is either 'a tramp who works' or 'a migratory worker, especially one who will work whenever he finds an opportunity', as we see from the 'American Tramp and Underworld Slang' of Godfrey Irwin, who suggests a derivation-by-corruption from *homo bonus*; to those who know that many cant words have a learned origin this seems a possibility. In ordinary colloquial use, *bo* is always a term of address; as a non-vocative, it is 'generally applied to all vagrants on railroad property by trainmen, railroad police, and officials' (Irwin).

Buddy is in common use, in reputable as in underworld American slang, for a mate, a companion, a good friend; compare *buddy-up*, to make friends. The word is almost certainly a corruption of the

English *butty*, recorded for 1790 in the sense of a fellow-worker or a mate ; as a mining middleman, it comes later ; in present-day English, *butty* is a miner's mate and occasionally employed as a vocative, but as a familiar vocative, not confined to miners, it had occurred as early as 1859 in Henry Kingsley's ' Geoffrey Hamlyn '. Three derivations have been proposed : *to play booty*, act as confederate, a phrase common enough in the seventeenth and eighteenth centuries (Weekley and ' The Oxford Dictionary ') ; *booty-pal*, Romany for a fellow-workman (Farmer) ; *buttock*, or rather the shortened *butt* (the latter current in dialect from at least as early as 1800), since in mining especially but also at other jobs men often work back to back (Irwin)—and was not a recent mining novel called ' The Back-to-Backs ' ? Despite the fact that dialect has the phrase *to play butty*, I ' vote for ' the third derivation, for the words are not necessarily identical.

RHYMING SLANG, BACK SLANG, AND OTHER ODDITIES

I

RHYMING slang appears to be a simple, straightforward theme. The practice of speaking in rhyming slang is easy, but the origin is obscure. John Camden Hotten, scholar and publisher, was the pioneer in the study of the subject. Writing in 1858, he told how, from inquiries made of patterers and chaunters or 'paper-workers' (that is, various types of that now almost extinct class, the itinerant vendors of ballads, dying speeches, confessions), he learnt that rhyming slang was introduced about 1843–5. I have reason to believe that it arose about 1830, was fairly common among London costermongers and their like at the period mentioned by Hotten, and that by 1860 it was general among the London poor.

At its inception, rhyming slang may, like cant, have been a 'secret' language; it soon lost its secrecy for the obvious reason that it presented no obstacle to the intelligent. Nevertheless, without actually knowing the vocabulary of rhyming slang, one might be puzzled as to which of several alternatives a given rhyming term was supposed to represent, and it is to this day true that the Cockney, or any other expert, can speak in comparative security by employing a slurred and rapid utterance of a mixture of rhyming slang with either back or centre slang or indeed with both. But costermongers, patterers and chaunters did not, even in the early days, have a monopoly of rhyming slang: compositors employed it freely, as one would expect of a body of men responsible for much remarkable slang; street boys soon picked it up and became proficient in its use.

But until 1914–18, rhyming slang was, except for a very superficial knowledge of it, confined to the poorer Cockney, to the small dealers and the newsvendors of the provinces (who got it from the Cockney), and to such emigrants to the Colonies as had known this slang before they left England. I remember that as a boy I knew about, and could clumsily handle, both back and centre slang (sometimes called terminal and medial slang), but I did not, except by name, know anything about rhyming slang. In 1914–18, like many another Englishman—whether from England or from the Colonies—I came into close contact with this amusing fashion of speech. Rhyming slang soon made itself an important and essential part of soldiers' slang, the more rapidly that a small proportion of rhyming slang already belonged to the specialized vocabulary of the Regular Army. It is therefore clear that while the vocabulary of the comparatively uneducated man was greatly enlarged by the strenuous promiscuities of 1914–18, the educated man likewise added considerably to his knowledge of English: there are not wanting critics that assert the gain of the latter to exceed the gain of the former.

Too often did the uneducated learn rather the vocabulary of journalism than that of a truly good English, whereas the educated heard many a vivid and many a forcible piece of dialect or slang, and many a simple, direct word for his own effete equivalent. But this is to leave the path of rhyming slang for the highway of ordinary speech : let us return to our Billy Buttons, I mean our muttons.

I shall not here develop my pet theory that rhyming slang arose from a slow accumulation of coincidences and accidents, for example the Warwickshire dialectal *holy friar* for a liar,[1] but pass to examples.

It has been remarked that ' the rhymes often indicate a religious upbringing or the memory of innocent nursery rhymes ', as in *Abraham's willing*, a shilling ; *Cain and Abel*, a table ; *Pope o' Rome*, a home. The predominantly London origin of rhyming slang is shown by the frequent presence of the metropolis in the group of terms based on topography, as in the following examples : *Bushey Park*, a lark ; *Camden Town*, a brown (slang for a halfpenny) ; *Chalk Farm*, the arm ; *Charing Cross*, a horse, where *Cross* is evidently pronounced, Cockney fashion, *crorse* ; *Covent Garden*, a farden, Cockney pronunciation for farthing ; *Hounslow Heath*, teeth ; *Isle of*

---

[1] Rhyming slang may well represent an amplification of scattered rhyming synonyms. The following appear in the eighteenth century : *bubbly Jock*, a turkey cock (slang and dialect) ; *cry beef*, thieves' cant for ' to cry *thief* ' ; *The dogs have not dined*, ' his shirt hangs out behind,' though this may be wholly accidental, and half a dozen others at least as early as 1780. See *passim* my edition of Grose's ' Vulgar Tongue '.

France, a dance; *Maidstone jailor*, a tailor; *River Lea*, tea; *St. Martin's-le-Grand*, the hand.

As large a group is formed from the names of famous or notorious persons. *Charley Lancaster*, a handkerchief, vulgarly handkercher; *Charley Prescott*, a waistcoat; *Duke of York*, either walk or talk as the occasion may be; *Jack* (sometimes *Harry*) *Randall*, a candle; *Joe Savage*, a cabbage; *Lord Lovel*, a shovel; *Rory o' More*, the floor; *Sir Walter Scott*, a pot (especially of beer); *Tommy o' Rann*, scran, low slang for food. All the preceding examples occur in Hotten's 'Slang Dictionary' (1874 edition), which gives a word now obsolete because the object is obsolete: *Lord John Russell*, a bustle.

Akin is the group referring to historical events or to periodical meetings or concourses of people; for instance, *Barnet fair*, hair; *Battle of the Nile*, a tile, a vulgarism for a hat; *Epsom races*, a pair of braces. Those examples are to be found in Hotten, and may still be heard occasionally to-day. Sometimes the term changes: in 1914–18, soldiers used *Jane Shore* for that wretched class which in 1870 was known as either *sloop of war* or *Rory o' More*. This last term, like *Duke of York*, illustrates the further fact that the one rhyming-slang term may stand for two or more words. Likewise the first member of a rhyming-slang phrase may appear in several others: *German band* is a hand (a word honoured with several rhyming equivalents), while *German flutes* (in 1914–18, *daisy roots*) are boots; *lean and lurch* is a church, *lean and fat* a hat; *oats and barley*, Charley; *oats and chaff*, path (i.e. a footpath); *sugar and honey*, money; *sugar-candy*, brandy.

The following examples are given as favourites among the soldiers in the Great War, with the caution that most of them existed long before. *Buckle my shoe*, a Jew ; *bushel and peck*, neck ; *cherry ripe*, a pipe ; *Dicky dirt*, a shirt ; *fire alarms*, arms ; *grasshopper*, a copper, i.e. a military policeman ; *half inch*, pinch, i.e. steal ; *Joanna*, a piano ; *Kate Karney*, the Army, such false rhymes being very frequent ; *loaf of bread*, either head or dead ; *plates of meat*, feet ; *squad, halt !*, salt ; *Tom Thumb*, rum ; *Uncle Ned*, bed ; *trouble and strife*, a wife ; *Wilkie Bards*,[1] a pack of cards.

Initiates, however, have long used abbreviations where possible, the general rule being that the truncated form should consist of two syllables ; *loaf* for *loaf of bread*, in the sense of head (never in that of dead), is an exception. Instead of *Bill is drunk*, the new hand will say *Bill's elephant's trunk*, but the old hand says tersely : *Bill's elephants*. The shamefaced newcomer might speak of his *Dicky dirt being bullock's horn* (his shirt being in pawn), while the expert would say : *My Dicky's bullocks* or even *my Dicky's bullocked*, the verb *to bullock* having arisen from the rhyming-slang phrase. When I enlisted, I was puzzled by someone asking : *Where's your chiner ?* On diligent inquiry I discovered that *chiner* was a slovenly pronunciation of *China* and that the latter represented *China plate*, which even to my limited understanding meant a mate, a friend. *Babbler* was Armyese for a

---

[1] For a whole set of rhyming-slang terms used in the game of House, see ' Songs and Slang of the British Soldier : 1914–1918 ', by John Brophy and the writer. (3rd edition, 1931, Oxford University Press.)

cook, *babbler* being a development from *babbling*, itself short for *babbling brook*. *Titfer* was short for *tit-for-tat*, a hat, and in 1914-18 it also conveyed very strong assent. The modern low slang *dooks* is a corruption of *dukes*, which abbreviates *Duke of Yorks*, which represents *forks*, which is slang for *fingers*, *fingers* being synecdoche for *hands*. This distinctly intelligent use of language originated with, and is most skilfully practised by, ' the lower orders ' : no unprejudiced judge will deny that it is very much more clever and attractive than schoolboy gibberish, including that heard at some of our great Public Schools.

The same process is seen in *lord*, an obsolescent term for a sixpenny piece : it is short for *lord of the manor*, obviously a ' tanner ' ; similarly, *touch-me* is now rarely heard for a shilling, but it abbreviates *touch me on the nob*, rhyming-slang for a ' bob '. (*Rogue and villain* is also obsolescent if not quite obsolete ; a shillin'.) A sailors' term is *old Jamaica*, for sun ; obviously short for *old Jamaica rum*, another instance of imperfect rhyme. An equally amusing soldiers' term is *o my !*, standing for *o my Gord !*, a sword.

II

The ' Oxford Dictionary ' is decorously brief on the subject of Back Slang. Having stated that the term derives from the adverb, it defines thus : ' A kind of slang in which every word is pronounced backwards ; as *ynnep* for *penny* ' ; the Dictionary then cites John Camden Hotten and quotes from Wheatley's informative book, ' Anagrams ', which remarks :

'Back Slang . . . is formed by the costermongers upon anagrammatical principles; thus *look* is *cool*.'

John Camden Hotten, for this as for many subjects connected with slang and colloquial speech, is the *locus classicus*, the chief authority, the best illustration. In 'The Slang Dictionary' (revised edition, 1874) we read: 'The costermongers of London number between thirty and forty thousand. Like other low tribes [from the Bohemian Hotten this is surprisingly "Victorian"], they boast a language, or secret tongue, by which they hide their designs, movements, and other private affairs. This costers' speech offers no new fact . . . for philologists; it is not very remarkable for originality of construction, neither is it spiced with low humour, as other cant. But the costermongers boast that it is known only to themselves; that it is far beyond the Irish, and puzzles the Jews. . . . It is now mostly spoken, mixed, however, with various other kinds of slang, in the public markets—the new dead-meat market being, perhaps, strongest in the way of pure . . . back slang.'

Back slang has always been peculiar to Cockneys, although they have not tried to confine it to London; back slang reached the Colonies—well, fifty years ago at least. But it has never been generally known either in England or abroad.

While it is true that the basis is the pronouncing of words backwards, this slang is not quite so simple as all that. Sometimes, to render pronunciation more easy, an additional syllable is tacked on—at either end; sometimes the word reversed is very different from what an uninitiated speaker might expect. When a coster has spelt out a longish word, even one of two or three syllables, in the normal order, it looks rather strange; when he spells it backwards, it becomes stranger still. For instance, *shilling* becomes *genitraf*, and this may be shortened to *gen*. Ordinary slang and cant words may be inserted into the back-slang sentence or conversation, and often these intrusions are converted into a back-slang form. Occasionally, if the word has three or more syllables, one or two of them retain their usual form. Words beginning with *h* often, in back slang, end with the substituted *ch*: hat becomes *tach* (pronounced *tatch*). In somewhat the same way, *half* becomes *flach* (pronounced *flatch*).

In 'kacab genals', the name given by initiates to back slang, there are several other refinements worth noting. To form a plural, *s* must be added: *woman* reads *nammow*, but *women* reads *nammows*. When a word does not admit of a direct reversion of its letters, letters change position in order to obtain some sort of euphony: *pound* becomes not *dnuop* but *dunop*. Also, as in the reversing of the words *back slang*, all one-syllabled words ending in two consonants are given two syllables: *long* turns into *genol*, *cold* into *deloc*, *drunk* into *kennurd*. A further variant is offered in *elrig*, instead of *lerig*, for *girl*, where the additional vowel is displaced from its normal position and made to begin the back-slang word. That additional vowel is always *e*.

Before passing to some specimens of back slang, it may be noted that this 'slanguage' is not confined to English: in Germania, the Spanish 'thieves' slang' or cant, and in Argot, the low slang of the French, the same trick was, and still is, practised.

Even in India, in the nineteenth century, an itinerant tribe of jugglers known as Bazeegars had a back slang based on Hindustani.

The following specimens serve to show that anyone equipped with both cant and back slang is able to talk in a way apt to confuse the 'new chum'.

Cool the delo nammow, beyond meaning literally 'look at the old woman', conveys to a fellow-costermonger or initiate the further fact that she is a nuisance; *da-erb* is bread; *edgabac* a cabbage; *ekom* a moke, a donkey; *emag*, game. *Esclop* is patently police, but is used of a specific constable; this piece of back slang has enriched general slang with 'slop', now obsolescent. *Fi-heath* denotes a thief, *hel-bat* a table. *Mur* is rum: perhaps the commonest of all back-slang words among soldiers taking part in the late national unpleasantness on the Western Front; so common that many used it without suspecting its origin. *Nevis stretch* is literally a seven-stretch, the latter word being cant for a lengthy imprisonment; hence the phrase means seven years' penal servitude. *Tenip* is a pint, and *top o' reeb* is a pot of beer. *Dab tros*, a bad sort, should be compared with *trosseno*, literally one sort, but actually bad. A quaintly relevant old slang phrase is *to back slang it*, to go out of the back door.

If back is sometimes called terminal slang, medial is occasionally used for centre slang. Centre slang is nowadays less frequently heard than back slang, and both are less frequent than rhyming slang. Centre slang is the most recent of the three; it is used less as a substitute for either of those other two varieties than as a further ingredient, often as a complication. The chief necessity, in speaking centre slang, is to take the central vowel of any word and to begin the new word with it; but one must also, or rather one usually does, add vowels and consonants to one's liking. Mug becomes *ugmer*; fool, *oolerfer*; flat, *atfler*. Any central slang word may have an *h* prefixed: e.g. *hugmer*. If the formation is rigid and regular, the result is tiresome in the extreme; but adepts have evolved some curious words, such as *evethee* for thief. Centre slang is more difficult than back slang and not nearly so amusing as rhyming slang; but all three will often serve to solve an otherwise insoluble piece of Cockney slang or of cant.

Not so very different is gibberish, which antedates rhyming, back, and centre slang by at least a century, and probably by two hundred years. Grose in 1796, in his famous dictionary of colloquialism, slang and cant, writes thus: 'A sort of disguised language, formed by inserting any consonant between each syllable of an English word; in which case it is called the gibberish of the letter inserted: if *F*, it is the F gibberish, if *G*, the G gibberish; as in the sentence, How do you do? Howg dog youg dog?' Hotten asserts that this 'old English mode of canting' was 'affected only by the most miserable impostors'. Originally the word gibberish meant the special lingo of gipsies and beggars, now it tends to mean any unintelligible or inarticulate nonsense. One of the most readable and sensible of the early lexicographers, Thomas Dyche, thus sketches the history of the word in his definition: 'An unintelligible jargon, or confused way of speaking, used by the gipsies, beggars,

&c., to disguise their wicked designs; also any discourse where words abound more than sense' (1748, or seven years before the publication of Dr. Johnson's dictionary). But the kind of gibberish mentioned by Grose has survived among schoolboys: I myself heard it in New Zealand in 1904–6. A variation is got by adding, not a consonant but a syllable—often *vis*. Hotten irritably remarks (with much justice if little urbanity): ' These things are worthy of schoolboys, as they [? the gibberish or the boys] are in ability far below the rhyming, the back, or the centre slang, each of which is constructed by people possessing no claim to literary excellence whatever.' Hotten interestingly adds that ' in 1823, when the Diorama created a sensation in Paris, . . . *on parlait en rama* '; i.e. one ended significant words with *rama*. He pertinently remarks that such adaptations ' can hardly be called slang, or we shall have everybody making a slang of his own '.

Closely related to the *howg dog youg dog* slang is that known as Ziph. (This word, like *Germania* and *centre slang*, is omitted by the ' Oxford Dictionary '.) Ziph consists in repeating every vowel or diphthong and inserting *g* between the two vowelled elements; the accent falls on the additional syllable. Thus: *Shagall wege gogo agawagay* signifies: Shall we go away? Obviously the answer to a question so conveyed is in the affirmative, while the inquirer should be in the infirmary. Hotten is again scornful: and again one must admit that his scorn is, in the main, justified. Yet Ziph has a history, which may be studied in three books that are as unlike one another as this essay of mine and a short story: Mansfield's

'School Life at Winchester College'; De Quincey's 'Autobiographic Sketches' (the Opium-Eater complacently pats himself on the back for remembering this simple gibberish); and in 1688 Bishop John Wilkins's 'Essay towards a Philosophic Language'.

THE ART OF LIGHTENING WORK

THIS is not an essay on the correct procedure for drawing the dole, but a verbal excursion into the realms of legitimate rest from work. There exists a group of words denoting the refreshment taken during these periods of repose: the delightfulness of the occasion probably has much to do with the interest, the vividness, the quaintness, and the singular aptness of the terms here treated; it is now recognized that the object, action, quality or occasion designated has greatly influenced the nature —the sound and the shape—of the word concerned. The study of words has, in short, become humanized, and there is an increasing public for 'etymological essays' and 'word histories'; the good work was begun by Richard Chenevix Trench, Archbishop of Dublin; the best present-day exponents of this provocative study are Mr. Logan Pearsall Smith and Professor Ernest Weekley.

Of the 'rest-refreshment' words here dealt with, four are well known, but the less familiar words are equally interesting. One belongs to the vocabulary of standard English, one used to be good English but is now obsolete except in dialect, one is much employed by residents in India, one is slang, while the remainder belong to dialect.

Snack is slang, though its less-known synonyms (*snap*

and *snatch*) are dialect. *Snack* is first recorded in 1402 in the sense of a snap, a bite ; in that of a share or portion,[1] in the second half of the seventeenth century, when also arose that of a small quantity of liquor ; the phrase *to go snacks*, to have a share, to divide profits, is found in Dryden in 1693, but it existed earlier as cant, as we see from B.E.'s ' Dictionary of the Canting Crew ', 1690 : ' *To go snacks*, to go halves or share and share alike. *Tip me my Snack, or else I'll Whiddle.* Give me my share, or I'll tell.' *Snack* as a light or an incidental meal originated about 1750, the actor-dramatist Foote being one of the first to use it.[2] Captain Francis Grose included it as a colloquialism in his entertaining ' Classical Dictionary of the Vulgar Tongue ', late in the eighteenth century. The word has long been used in dialect, which has several senses peculiar to itself, Scottish possessing the picturesque *make snacks of*, to devour. It has also been slang for perhaps a century and as such it is recorded in John Camden Hotten's ' Slang Dictionary ', as well as in Farmer and Henley's ' Slang and its Analogues ' ; the ' Concise Oxford ', which notes the Middle Dutch *snakken*, to snap, does not, however, describe it as slang ; nor does Wyld's excellent ' Universal Dictionary of the English Language ', which notes that the sense of ' share ' is obsolete and that even Pope used the phrase, *to go snacks*.

[1] As simply a part, the word occurs in Captain John Stevens's manly and competent Spanish dictionary, 1726.

[2] For dates and earliest recordings I am, inevitably, heavily indebted to the (in every sense) great ' Oxford English Dictionary ', whose findings I am proud to be able, occasionally, to supplement.

Strictly analogous and almost alternative are the cognate *snap* and *snatch*. *Snap* in the sixteenth century was cant for a share and in the eighteenth *go snaps* was synonymous with *go snacks* ; as a hasty meal it came a century earlier than *snack* and was thus used by the worthy Fuller ; in the nineteenth century, when it was also mining slang, George Eliot used it colloquially. A sidelight on this sense of a slight, irregular meal that is hardly a meal is thrown by the standard English *snaps*, ' kinds of small crisp cake ',[1] for example, of gingerbread (*ginger snaps*). The word is of either Scandinavian or Dutch origin.[2] Unlike *snack*, *snap* has disappeared from colloquial English to linger in dialect, and this applies almost as much to *snatch*, which Boswell records in his ' Tour to the Hebrides ' and which, in the sense of a hasty meal, appears as early as Tusser (1573).

Lunch is earlier—and has always been less formal—than *luncheon* ; the latter appears in Browning's *Pied Piper of Hamelin* :

> So munch on, crunch on, take your nuncheon,
> Breakfast, supper, dinner, luncheon.

Nuncheon, the earliest, is now obsolete ; it comes from the Middle English *none-chenche*, noon draught ; *chenche* was a debased form from Anglo-Saxon *scencan*, to pour. The words *luncheon* and *lunch* date from the sixteenth century, when they denoted a hunk, a piece ; the origin is almost certainly the Spanish *lonja*, which Minsheu in 1617 defines by implication as a piece, for he gives *lonja* as ' *quidquid porrigit sese in longitudinem* ',

---

[1] ' Concise Oxford ', revision of 1931.
[2] See especially Wyld's ' Universal Dictionary ', 1932.

THE ART OF LIGHTENING WORK

and he glosses *lonja de torcino* as 'a lunch of bacon'. *Lunch* as a piece, a hunk, lasted in general use till late in the eighteenth century. Stevens in 1726 defines *lonja* as 'lunch'—in Spanish *lonja* has never signified a meal. But *lunch* as a meal dates only from about 1820, while *luncheon* in the same sense originated about 1650. At first, and for long, *luncheon* meant a snack taken between two regular meals, especially and almost solely a snack eaten between breakfast and midday dinner. But in Suffolk *luncheon* was a light repast eaten in the afternoon; in various dialects both *luncheon* and *lunch* have survived as a large piece, especially of food, especially again if the food be meat, bread or cheese. *Nuncheon*, variant *nunch*, is in much more general dialectal use, either as lunch or as a fore- or afternoon snack. *Nuncheon*, the form and the sense of which affected those of *luncheon*, dates from the fourteenth century, at first a very light repast of liquor and food taken in the afternoon and until the seventeenth century usually ending in *s*; the spellings have always varied greatly, but the *-ks* forms went out with the sixteenth century, towards the end of which the *-eon*, *-ion* forms became the most general. In 1611, Florio in his Italian dictionary defines *merenda* as 'a nunchin, a bever, an anders-meate, a repaste between dinner [at 2 or 3 o'clock] and supper', *merendare* as 'to eat between dinner and supper, to nunchin', and *merendina* as 'a little or hungry nunchin'. Cotgrave in the same year, in his French dictionary, defines *gouster* as 'a nunchion, drinking, aunders-meat, afternoones-collation, mouthes-recreation', and *collation de moyne* as 'a Monks nuncheon; as much as another man eats at a large meale'; *manger son pain en son sac* is, ' to snudge, it, or muncheon it alone in a corner ', an example antedating the ' Oxford Dictionary's ' record by fifty-five years ; this form of the word is probably from *munch* on the analogy of *nunchin*, *-eon*, &c., and has an ' intriguing ' parallel in the nineteenth-century dialectal *munch*, a (usually light) meal.

Much less general, confined indeed to Scottish and Northern dialect, is *nacket* or *nocket*, a snack or even a lunch ; a word not recorded before 1789. Cognate, apparently, is Scottish *nackie*, a loaf of bread, a small cake, for we find *nocket* used in the same sense in Roxburghshire.

Slang, not dialect, has given us *tiffin*, which undoubtedly comes from *tiffing*, the verbal noun from *tiff*, to drink slowly, to sip, recorded first for 1769 ; Grose (1785) has *tiffing*, ' eating or drinking out of meal time. . . . A tiff of punch,[1] a small bowl of punch.' *Tiffin*(*g*), which, unlike the verb *tiff*, does not find a place in dialect, early migrated to India, where it came to mean the midday meal ; rather more of an ' institution ' than the English lunch, as the quotations in the valuable ' Hobson-Jobson '[2] serve to show. In the present century, the residents in India have tended, however, to make tiffin a light meal : knowledge of healthy dieting has greatly increased since Queen Victoria's reign. It may perhaps be added that in New Zealand, during the years 1902–7, the writer often heard *tiffin* used of a very light repast taken in either the fore- or the afternoon during a ten minutes' rest from work : tea with either bread-and-butter or scones or cake.

[1] This phrase arose at least thirty years earlier.
[2] Yule and Burnell : ' Hobson-Jobson, A Glossary of Colloquial Anglo-Indian ', revised by W. Crooke, 1903.

THE ART OF LIGHTENING WORK 47

The next four terms—*damper, doggy, biting-on, piece*—are very little known to anyone unfamiliar with dialect; none has succeeded in gaining the citizenship of standard English. Three have remained wholly dialectal, while one (*damper*) has gone half-way to enfranchisement by being at one period used in colloquial speech, and another (*piece*) has, though never emerging from dialect, had a development in the United States. *Damper*, says Grose—this forestalls the ' Oxford English Dictionary ' by twenty years—is ' a luncheon, or snap before dinner ; so called from its damping or allaying the appetite ' ; the O.E.D. entry is from Maria Edgeworth, ' in the kitchen, taking his snack by way of a damper '. As a lunch or a snack, the word is found in Lancashire but not, apparently, in any other dialect ; as a colloquialism it survived until 1891 at least ; compare, too, the schoolboys' nineteenth-century use for ' a suet pudding served before meat '[1] and the Australian use for ' a large scone of flour and water baked in hot ashes ; the bread of " the bush ", which is always unleavened ', though in the latter the damping of the flour probably accounts for the origin of the term.[2]

Doggy (not recorded in the O.E.D.) is restricted to Suffolk, where it means—or has until recently meant —' a snack or drink taken by harvesters, &c., between meals ', an explanation found only in the ' English Dialect Dictionary ', so self-sacrificingly compiled by the late jovial and astonishing Joseph Wright, whom to know was to love. Likewise only in the E.D.D. is

[1] Farmer and Henley, *op. cit.*
[2] Edward E. Morris, ' Austral English ', 1898 ; a book too little known.

biting-on, either a 'light refreshment taken between meals' or 'lunch'; the earliest record is for 1869 and the term is confined to Yorkshire, Lancashire, and Derbyshire. The related *bite and sup*, however, is common in Scotland (Scott has it in 1819, Crockett in 1895), Northumberland and Cumberland, Yorkshire and Staffordshire and Lincolnshire. Cognate too is *bite*, noun and verb, (to eat) a small portion of food, a term that has travelled as far south as Essex.

Better known is *piece*, long used (first record, about 1787) in Scottish and English dialect as short for 'piece of bread', generally with butter, and especially if eaten by itself as a snack; the E.D.D., however, says that the term is applied chiefly to such a slice 'given to children and carried in the pocket, to be eaten as lunch'; hence, *piece-time* is lunch-time. In the United States, *eat a piece* or just *piece* formerly meant ' to eat between meals ', but it is obsolescent.

We now come to three terms based on the morning hours : *ten-o'clock*, *elevener* or *elevens*, and *twelve-hours*. In Howitt's ' Rural Life ', 1838, we find the instructive sentence, ' Betty mean-time has put up their " luncheons " or " ten-o'clocks ",' which leads to the E.D.D.'s definition : ' slight refreshment taken about ten o'clock, esp. by labourers in the field '. Variants are *ten-hours' bite*, used by Burns (whereas *ten-o'clock* is North Country), and that other Scottish term *ten-hours*, which is, however, applied only to ' a slight feed given to horses while in the yoke in the forenoon ' (E.D.D.). These are still in use, as are *elevens* [1] and the alternatives, *elevener*, *eleven hours*, and *eleven o'clock(s)* ;

[1] Given by the ' Concise Oxford '.

THE ART OF LIGHTENING WORK 49

all these *eleven* [1] terms are dialectal, *eleven hours* being Scottish, *eleven o'clock(s)* belonging to Warwickshire and Somersetshire, *elevener* to South Scotland (as in Wilson's 'Tales', 1836) and the southern counties of England,[2] and *elevens* to Worcestershire, Gloucestershire, Dorsetshire, Kent and Suffolk.[3] For all, the meaning is 'a slight meal or refreshment taken by labourers, &c., in the forenoon' (E.D.D.). *Twelve-o'clock* represents the ordinary midday meal, and only in Leicestershire, but *twelve-hours* is either lunch or any other refreshment taken at noon ; *twelve-hours*, which has the variant forms *twal-hours, twull-hoors*, and *twull oors*, is Scottish and has been current since about the beginning of the last century.

But the most interesting term of all is *beaver* or *bever*, which is not to be found in 'Chambers', the 'Concise Oxford', or the 'Universal'. It has long been extant only in slang and dialect. As slang, it was common in the nineteenth century, often in the form of *bevvy* : in Hotten's 'Slang Dictionary' we find '*Bivvy*, or *gatter*, beer ; " shant of bivvy ", a pot or quart of beer ', which sense reappears in the English soldiers' slang of the War : Fraser and Gibbons, in their full and valuable 'Soldier and Sailor Words and Phrases', give it as *bevvy*, 'Beer. Any drink. (Beverage).' Yet the 'beverage' sense has been obsolete in standard speech for almost two centuries, nor can we describe the *bever* of Eton, Westminster, and Winchester as standard. At these three public schools,[4] during

[1] Only *elevener* and *elevens* appear in the O.E.D.
[2] Cornwall has also a shortened form : *levener*.
[3] Kent and Suffolk have also the derivative *elevenses*.
[4] Where it was abolished c. 1890.

the nineteenth century, it signified ' an afternoon meal served in hall ', and while at Eton [1] the spelling was either *beaver* or *beever*, that at Winchester was *beever*.[2] Mansfield, in ' School-life at Winchester College ', 1870, writes : ' In summer time we were let out of afternoon school for a short time about 4 p.m., when there was a slight refection of bread and cheese laid out in Hall. It was called *beever-time*, and the pieces of bread *beevers*.' Somewhat the same was true of Charterhouse, where, ' if a boy wants an additional piece of bread, he asks for a " beavor ", a bit taken with drink '.[3] In dialect, *beaver* in one of its many forms [4] is very general in the Midlands and Southern Counties,[5] and, whereas it only occasionally means a regular midday meal, it generally means ' slight refreshment [6] taken between meals, either at 11 a.m. or 4 p.m.' (E.D.D.) ; more often applied to the morning than the afternoon snack. In Cussans's ' History of Hertfordshire ' (1880), we read that the labourers' meals are ' first breakfast, before 6 ; breakfast, or eight o'clock, at 8 ; beaver at 10 or 11 '. *Bever-time* (a term confined to Bedfordshire and Suffolk) therefore signified a fore- or afternoon interval allowed for refresh-

[1] Farmer and Henley.

[2] In literary and general use (i.e. until *c.* 1730) *bever* is the norm.

[3] ' Public Schools Calendar ', 1886, cited by E.D.D.

[4] *Bever, beaver, bevor, beever, baver, baiver* ; in Northants sometimes corrupted to *maver*.

[5] In Kent, *beaver* is heard near Sittingbourne ; but the true Kentish word is *'lowance*, though elsewhere this word means ' an allowance of food and ale or its equivalent in money given to labourers in addition to wages ' (E.D.D.).

[6] Beer with bread-and-cheese has always been the usual form.

THE ART OF LIGHTENING WORK

ment; a *bever-cake* (Suffolk only), ' a cake made to eat with ale, at 4 p.m.'

Like *nuncheon* and *tiffin*, *bever* originally meant drink or drinking, then food and drink, then a repast. It is first recorded for 1451 in the famous Paston Letters, but even the ' light refreshment ' sense dates from as early as 1499 in that invaluable glossary, the ' Promptorium Parvulorum ' ; it recurs in such late sixteenth-century dictionaries as Cooper's ' Thesaurus ' and the ' Nomenclator ' : in the ' Promptorium ', *merendula* is defined as ' a bever after none ' and *bever* itself as ' drinking time ' ; in the ' Thesaurus ', we find *merenda* to be ' a collation, a noone meale, a boyver ' (Middle French, *boivre*), and in the ' Nomenclator ' we meet with the illuminating ' a middaies meale : an undermeale : a boire or beaver : a refreshing betwixt meales '. (The beginning of the seventeenth century witnessed the rise of the verb *bever*, which did not outlive the eighteenth century.) The seventeenth-century dictionaries show that this was the ' golden age ' of *bever* in general speech and writing. Cotgrave and Florio, both in 1611, have already been quoted ; [1] the word is, of course, from Old French *beivre*,[2] to drink ; Latin *bibere*. Minsheu, in his literally marvellous ' Ductor in Linguas . . . The Guide into the Tongues ', 1617, defines *bever* as ' drinking betweene meales ' and traces the etymology back to the Hebrew. Henry Hexham, in his Dutch dictionary, 1660, has ' a Beaver before supper ' and ' to beaver, or to drinke betweene meales '. John Ray's ' Dictionariolum Tri-

[1] See paragraph on *nuncheon*.
[2] The fifteenth- and sixteenth-century English spellings vary greatly.

lingue', which consists of classified lists of English words with the Latin and Greek, gives *beaver* as a meal between (midday) dinner and supper and glosses it as *merenda;* in almost every sixteenth-eighteenth-century Latin-English dictionary, moreover, the word *merenda* will be glossed as *be(a)ver.* B.E.'s cant dictionary, 1690, defines *bever* as 'an afternoon's Lunchion'. For the eighteenth century we need cite only two instances. Captain John Stevens in his Spanish dictionary, 1726, explains *colación* as 'a collation, that is, a repast of cold meat, or rather what is allow'd on a fasting night, a *bever,* an evening-meal . . .'; *merienda* as 'an afternoon's luncheon, a cold entertainment; a bever', and in the terser English-Spanish part he somewhat inconsistently lists *to bever* as 'to drink between meals' and the noun as 'drinking between meals'—but then Stevens was a very independent sort of fellow! Grose in his 'Vulgar Tongue' (1st edition, 1785, but to be consulted in the much fuller 3rd edition) defines as 'an afternoon's luncheon'.

But this makes thirsty reading . . .

THE PHILOLOGY OF CHRISTMAS

THIS is not an attempt to compete with the chosen ones of the kingdom of elysian etymology : Skeat, Sweet, Wright, Platt and other mighty men before the Lord of Language would probably rush to the gates of their privileged precincts and shoo me off quite rudely. But there are, concerning the essential phraseology of Christmas, some interesting facts and conjectures that quite well-educated persons have entirely forgotten or never encountered.

The very words *Christmas Eve* are misleading, for many think of them as the evening of the 24th December, whereas they would more accurately think of them as the whole of the day before Christmas, *eve* being here the day before. *Christmas-tide* and *Yule-tide* (this latter was the earlier term) refer not properly to Christmas Eve, Christmas Day and Boxing Day (though this is the modern usage), but to the fourteen days beginning with Christmas Eve, for in the Middle Ages there was a festival period that, commencing strictly on Christmas Day, lasted twelve days in all; but as Christmas Eve was 'a spoilt day', so the first day after the boisterous and vinous dozen was marked by half-hearted work and generous hours. In North Lincolnshire dialect, the same idea was and, though the term is now obsolescent, still is approximately conveyed by *Boxing-Time*, all the period from Christmas Day till the end of the first week in January.

Christmas itself, as many religious persons neglect to realize, is *Christ's Mass*, though actually there are three masses observed, the first being at midnight on Christmas Eve : this midnight mass is one of the ' sights ' of Paris. As so often happens in the study of words, *Christmas* is much more interesting in dialect than in refined and sometimes over-sophisticated ' good English ', for the pretty obvious reason that old festivals, customs, practices, and superstitions endure and survive much longer in the country than in the town. The word has at least twenty different dialectal forms, such as *Christenmass*, *Kersmas*, *Kessamus* ; it is used, especially in the phrase *the Christmas*, for the Christmas holidays. In Burne's fascinating ' Folk-Lore ', 1883, we read how the Shropshire people used to say that such and such a thing happened ' in the Christmas ', ' before Christmas was out ', or ' between the two Christmases ', i.e. between Christmas Day and Old Christmas Day (January 6, for the significance of which it is advisable to consult the ' Encyclopaedia Britannica ', or, better still, Duchesne's ' Christian Worship '). Burne tells how, even at that date, ' one special care was putting away any suds or bucklee for washing purposes, both of which it was most unlucky to keep in the house during " the Christmas ". . . . Some, also, put away leaven out of their houses. . . . The horses might not go to plough during the whole twelve days, nor might any spinning be done ; and the distaff, set aside, was not uncommonly dressed with flowers '.

This sense of *Christmas* has its derivative *Christmassing*, which means not only the Christmas holidays but the observance of Christmas, an evergreen employed in the Christmas decking of church or house, a Christmas present—and the begging for such a present. *Christmas* itself means Christmas evergreens, especially holly ('penn'orths of Christmas' is a Cornish phrase); and also a cake made by a courageous housewife or an affable cook on Christmas Eve. The following compound words are all linked up with some quaint custom intimately connected with the olden English Christmas and still remembered and, in isolated parts, still practised: *Christmas-block* or *-brand* or *-mock* or *-stock*, the Yule log; *Christmas-ball* or *-bo*, the desirable pudding; *Christmas-boys*, the young men acting in the rustic Christmas play; *Christmas-candle*, presented by grocers to each customer at Christmas-tide; *Christmas-pot*, a kind of alms consisting of spiced cake, good cheese, and mulled ale; *Christmas-shaf*, a sheaf of corn given on Christmas morning to every cow and horse—doubtless an allusive tribute to the glory of a certain manger and one of those homely-charming rites which crop up every now and then in the country; and the *Christmas-tree*, the holly. On some of these terms an essay could, but will not, be written.

Noel, the French of course for Christmas, came into England with the Normans and appears in Middle English for Christmas Day, Christmas-tide, a Christmas carol, and occasionally for Christ himself; the word survives as a Christian name. The anglicized form is *Nowel* or *Nowell*, a baptismal name that has become a surname. *Noel* is from the Latin *natalis (dies)*, birthday, and is connected with the birthday festival of Sol Invictus (the Latinized equivalent for Mithra, the Persian god of the Sun) held at Rome on December the 25th and partly responsible for both the date and the nature of Christmas ; from the Romance-languages form, *natal,* comes the South African province of Natal, which was discovered on Christmas Day. Significantly, neither *Noel* nor *Nowel(l)* can be found in dialect, which is notorious for its powers of resistance to foreign invasion : although it contains many successful gate-crashers.

Like *Nowell, Yule* and *Midwinter*—two other old names for Christmas—have become surnames and interesting members of the group derived from baptismal names suggested by the great Church festivals. *Yule* comes from the northern countries, as does the feast, which was a wholly pagan celebration at the winter solstice and later ' commandeered ' by Christian missionaries for the use of the Church. Etymologists in the last century derived from *Yule* our adjective *jolly*. Professor Ernest Weekley—to whom I owe many of the ' points ' made here—says that ' this is very doubtful . . . and intensive senses, e.g. *jolly good hiding, jolly well mistaken,* can be paralleled in Modern French '. It is true that in the Middle Ages one finds the form of *jolif,* that *joli* is used in the famous ' Sir Gawain and the Green Knight ' (*c.* 1400) for ' gay ', and that *jolilé* occurs in the same poem for ' bravely ', ' gallantly ', yet in many of the modern French phrases, *joli* retains the sense of ' pretty ' and *joliment* of ' prettily '. In 1923, watching Cochet play a lawn-tennis match with Darsonval the professional, I heard, not once but several times, the

THE PHILOLOGY OF CHRISTMAS

exclamation *joliment bien joué* (which I won't quibble to twist with a comma after *joliment*), but also an admiring *joli!* or *joli coup* (i.e. de raquette) ! Without wishing to run counter to so eminent an authority as Professor Weekley, I yet believe that the odds on *Yule* and *joli* are about even. In dialect the field is less disputable, and, there, *Yule* is a very common word : we even find *to Yule*, to observe Christmas or to participate in Christmas feasting. Eighteenth-century Scotland had the quaint proverb : ' It is crying Yule under another man's stool ', indicative of the spending of other people's money. Some of the *Yule* compounds are picturesque : *Yule-blinker*, the Christmas Star ; *Yule-crush*, a Christmas feast ; *Yule-dough*, any and every kind of Christmas pastry ; *Yule-e'en*, Christmas Eve ; *Yule-night*, Christmas night, hence a merry evening ; *Yule-play*, a holiday at Christmas.

Some of the ancient and modern appurtenances of Christmas are no less curious. *The Yule Log*, now embalmed in Christmas Annuals for the very young, burns low and is nigh to extinction, but once it was the cynosure of the revellers on Christmas Eve : a jolly survival of Scandinavian paganism. *Waits*, originally watchmen (municipal night-police), came, late in the eighteenth century, to mean Christmas minstrels : the primary sense of *wait* is to stand on guard. *Carol* either is derived from the old French *carole*, a specific form of round dance, or is a development from *chorus* influenced by *carole*. The earliest extant carol is in Anglo-Norman of the thirteenth century ; it shows a pleasant regard for ' English ale ' and ' Gascon wine and French . . . and

Anjou's too'. As for *Holly*, *Ivy* and *Mistletoe*, they are survivals of Northern heathenism, the mistletoe being that sacred and mysterious Druidic plant which so frightened people that they did not use it as a pretext for kissing until early in the last century. *The Boar's Head*, once an essential of the Christmas feast, now adorns the sign of innumerable inns. The medieval *Lord of Misrule*, director of Christmas jollifications, went out with the second Stuart King of England and returned with Scott in 1820; the period of misrule was perhaps suggested by the duration of the Roman Saturnalia. *Wassail and Drinkhail*, in their original meanings, as toast and response, of *be well* (i.e. 'good health!') and *drink hale* (i.e. 'Thanks, I return the compliment—like a man'), now belong to the historical novel of an avoided period; but *wassail* remains, with the meanings 'a carousal', 'a drinking song', 'to hold a festive meeting'. *Pantomimes* are the modern secular equivalent of the medieval sacred plays, by way of the transitional masques that became so popular from about 1600; moreover, the pantomime, once silent, is now vocal enough for the most robust wassailer. *Christmas Boxes* were originally receptacles for the vails of servants and were opened for the common weal on the 26th of December.[1] Among those above-stairs, gifts were in the Middle Ages presented usually at the New Year, and in the twelfth century Jocelyn of Brakelonde, in his Chronicle, mentions this as a characteristically English custom: but I fear that the custom came from Rome. Gift-giving was pretty generally changed to Christmas Day when Queen

[1] See also Appendix I.

Victoria brought the *Christmas Tree* from Germany (where it arose in the eighteenth century) and inflicted it on her official household. She knew what she wanted, and we English got it.

ALL FOOLS' DAY

I REMEMBER that when I was about ten, I watched a local cricket match in New Zealand. Having come from the country, I knew little of guile, so that when someone asked me to take a bag out to the bowler, I readily did so : in fact, I was proud to be of use. The bowler sent me to the wicket-keeper, and the wicket-keeper sent me to the devil. Realizing that I had been ' had ', I strolled back to the small pavilion and returned the bag to the ' donor ' with the remark : ' That's for you to put your fat head in '—and I slipped quickly out of his reach. That form of April Fool is rarely practised nowadays ; but I shall never forget how wretched I felt at the moment of realization and how bitter when jeers greeted me as I reached the pavilion again. I suppose that, dimly, I thought : ' This isn't fair, for it's making a mock of good-nature and the readiness to help.' But the lesson was salutary ; and many another credulous, too-easy-going person has learnt a valuable lesson on April Fool Day.

The practice of fooling people on the first of April is not confined to any one country. Its origin is unknown. That similar tricks are played in India at the Huli Festival of the thirty-first of March is interesting but does not help very much.

The explanations, though inconclusive—if not worse

than inconclusive, are entertaining : like most explanations, they reveal more of the human mind than of the thing to be explained. One theory is that the practice began when Noah dispatched the questing dove before the flood had subsided ; this he did on the first day of that month which answers to our April. To perpetuate the memory of the final emergence from the Ark, it was considered desirable that whosoever forgot this remarkable occurrence should be sent on some sleeveless errand similar to that upon which Noah sent the unfortunate bird.

One of the most far-fetched explanations is that All Fools' or April Fool Day commemorates Christ's enforced pillar-to-post ' journeying ' from Annas to Caiaphas, from Caiaphas to Pilate, from Pilate to Herod, and from Herod back again to Pilate. The Crucifixion took place about the first of April. But, in silliness, that explanation must yield to the theory advanced in one of the earliest of English periodicals, 'The British Apollo', in 1708. The Romans, it appears, wanted, soon after Rome was founded, to find wives, and carried off the Sabine women. This ' solution ' was ridiculed in a later issue of the same periodical :

> Ye witty sparks, who make pretence
> To answer questions with good sense,
> How comes it that your monthly Phoebus
> Is made a fool by Dionysus ?
> For had the Sabines, as they came,
> Departed with their virgin fame, . . .
> The girls had been the April Fools.
> Therefore, if this be'nt out of season,
> Pray think, and give a better reason.

What seems pretty sure is that April foolery is a

relic of the once very general festivities observed at the vernal equinox, the period beginning on the twenty-fifth of March (New Year's Day in the Old Style) and ending on the first of April. At Paris there had long been a Festival of Fools : such a legacy from Paganism as partook much rather of the nature of the Roman Saturnalia than of the milder, more sporadic pranks that became popular when France, the first European country to do so, adopted the reformed calendar ; the wags continued to send, to those who abided by the old calendar, silly or offensive presents disguised as genuine New Year gifts. It was probably from France that the custom infected the rest of Europe. In France, by the by, an April Fool is a *poisson d'avril*, an April fish, the phrase being explained in two ways : in April the sun leaves the zodiacal region of the fish (ingenious but improbable) ; an April fish is a young fish, therefore easily caught (more likely).

The custom reached England in the latter part of the seventeenth century. Its manifestations are as numerous as wit or malice can devise. I shall confine myself to what may be considered as ' historical '.

In Scotland the favourite form was, and is, to send a person from place to place with a letter, in which is written :

> On the first day of April
> Hunt the gowk another mile.

In some parts of Britain the reply to these very, or to equivalent, words would be :

> The gowk and the titline [or titlark] sits on a tree,
> Ye're a gowk as well as me.

The titlark is said to provide for the universally contemptuous cuckoo. That *gowk* in these two sets of verses means cuckoo and not fool is fairly certain, and that *April gowk* is the Scottish for *April fool* does not affect the question; the cuckoo is notoriously hard to 'hunt', i.e. track down.

A gibe heard in some parts, though it is dying out gradually, is:

> Fool, fool, April fool,
> You learn nought by going to school.

Once it is noon, of course, the biter is automatically the bitten, and a pleasant old reply to the would-be fooler runs thus:

> April Fool's gone past,
> You're the biggest fool at last;
> When April Fool comes again,
> You'll be the biggest fool then.

Several forms of the deception may be mentioned. In Grose's ' Classical Dictionary of the Vulgar Tongue ', 1785, I find this entry: ' APRIL FOOL. Any one imposed on, or sent on a bootless errand on the first of April, on which day it is the custom among the lower people, children and servants, by dropping empty papers carefully doubled up, sending persons on absurd messages, and such-like contrivances, to impose on every one they can, and then to salute them with the title of April-fool.'

In old-time London, one performed the ceremony of *washing the white lions*, and all over England, until about 1914, it was a common trick to send a child to bring a pint of pigeon's milk; from this hoary old dodge comes the eighteenth-century phrase, *to milk the pigeon*, to attempt the impossible ; that phrase is also connected with *to milk the bull*, to risk a foregone failure. Children and youths were long asked *to fetch a pint of strap oil*,[1] while adults might be invited *to dance Moll Dixon's round*, a picturesque thought that survived till near the end of the nineteenth century ; or they might be sent to buy a copy of 'The History of Eve's Mother'—if anyone succeeds in purchasing this delectable book, I place it on record that I shall be delighted to take it off his hands.

Many of the dialect phrases and terms are more vivid than the urban ones connected with this abstruse subject. In the North Country an *April-errand* or (showing Scottish influence) *gowk's errand* is that on which one is sent on the first of April. Variants of *April-fool* are *April-gawby* (Cheshire and Warwickshire), *April-gob* (Cheshire and Derbyshire), *April-gobby* (Cheshire again : oh, they're wags up there !), *April-gowk* (North Country), and *April-noddy* (Lancashire, where they have the pleasing rhyme :

> April-noddy's past an' gone,
> An' thou's a noddy for thinkin' on).

An April gowk has for over a century been equivalent, in Scotland, to a fool or a simpleton, and Scott himself says that the canny Scots 'make April gouks of you Cockneys every month in the year' ('The Fortunes of Nigel', 1822). There, too, *hunt a gowk* has always been the exclamation on making an April fool, and the phrase is even used metaphorically to mean a disappointment, while thus to befool anyone is *to*

---

[1] The French equivalent was *huile de coudre*, for which more than one obliging Tommy issued forth in 1915–18.

ALL FOOLS' DAY

hunt the gowk : relevant is that eloquent idiom, *to see the gowk in one's sleep*, to imagine a non-existent evil or non-existent piece of good fortune, to tend to have baseless fears or hopes ; also to repent, to think better of something. One other phrase is notable : *to hunt the glaiks*, sometimes *to get the glaiks* (literally, deceptions), is used in Scotland to indicate going on a sleeveless errand or being tricked ; only rarely was it applied specifically to April-fooling.

Addendum

One likes to recall the Wykehamist practice of sending a new boy to the most incongruous people for a 'pempe', which eventually turns out to be a piece of paper inscribed πέμπε (τὸν) μῶφον πρότερον (keep the fool moving !). I believe the custom has died out : if this is so it is a pity, for it was a good and quick way of teaching the child his way about the place, even though it probably originated in mere foolery.

REPRESENTATIVE NAMES [1]

ALTHOUGH mixed actions of ejectment were abolished by law in 1852, the names John Doe and Richard Roe, which represented the fictitious lessee of the plaintiff and the no less fictitious defendant in a fictitious lawsuit taken as typical of all such suits, have survived. Nowadays, they provide a convenient method of typifying *any* plaintiff and defendant; they are even, though loosely, heard sometimes as type-names for the layman in any official connexion whatsoever. The law's loss has been language's gain: a particular instance of a feature common to the development of language is this disappearance of some technicality that then becomes generalized to the more wholesome uses of ordinary speech. The famous eighteenth-century lawyer, Sir William Blackstone (1723–80), was, in 1768, the first to employ the phrase in the third volume of his great work, the ' Commentaries on the Laws of England ', which, owing to its lucid arrangement and most perspicuous style, remains the best general history of this subject and is indeed a classic of our English tongue. Other notable literary instances of the use of these coupled names occur in Samuel Warren's extremely successful novel, ' Ten Thousand a Year ' (1841), and

[1] Cf. ' On Calling Names ', in Professor Weekley's delightful volume, ' Words and Names '.

Dean 'Eric, or Little by Little' Farrar's book on 'Early Christianity' (1882).

John Doe and Richard Roe, 'born' about the middle of the eighteenth century, were the heirs of John-a-Nokes and John- or Tom-a-Stiles, except that the earlier terms were, in law, used in a rather more general sense, for John-a-Nokes was one party to *any* lawsuit, John-a-Stiles was the other. Moreover, the older terms did not die out until about 1820 : we find Sir Walter Scott, in 1815, using *John a' Nokes* as equivalent to any individual member of the lower classes. An interesting survival of the old couple is that in Charles Clark's 'John Noakes and Mary Stiles', which, published in 1839, is a poem dealing with the visit of an Essex man—' an Essex Calf' was the jocularly depreciative phrase of the time—to the Tiptree races ; this poem purported to exhibit 'some of the lingual localisms peculiar to Essex' and had a glossary, and evidently it was authentic, for the late Professor Skeat, whom it would have taken more than the humorous Clark to hoodwink, included it in his 'Five Specimens of English Dialects', 1895. A very interesting sidelight on the transition is afforded by Captain Francis Grose of the Militia—an antiquary of exceptional ability, a wag of note, a lexicographer of point and wit—in his 'Dictionary of the Vulgar Tongue' (1785) : 'NOKES. A ninny, or fool. John-a-Nokes and Tom-a-Stiles ; two honest peaceable gentlemen, repeatedly set together by the ears by lawyers of different denominations, but now very seldom, having for several years past been supplanted by two other honest peaceable gentlemen, namely, John Doe and Richard Roe.' *Tom-a-Stiles* appeared some thirteen years earlier in the 'comic and satyrical poems' of G. A. Stevens, who, undoubtedly one of the (less savoury) 'characters' of his century, is now known only to scholars and to readers of what the booksellers so charmingly call 'curiosa'; *John*-a-Stiles, however, arose more than two centuries earlier, is recorded in Sir Philip Sidney's noble apology for poetry (1581), and first in a document of fifty years earlier, the 'Dialogue on the Laws of England', where we find mention also of one *Johan at Noke*, this, like *John an Okes, John at Noke, John of the Nokes*, &c., &c., being a variant form. The original of the latter was *John atten Oke*, John at the Oak, that tree being close by his place of residence; John-a-Stiles, on the other hand, was variously called *John at Stile, John of the Stile*, &c., and his name represents *John atte Stile*, John (who lives) at the stile. These two names are examples of the surnames-from-places so common that one is only too apt to forget their often 'intriguing' origin. That they had won a further fame as early as the Commonwealth appears in a quotation from Howell's book on Foreign Travel: 'Nor indeed is he capable to beare any Rule or Office in Town or Countrey, who is utterly unacquainted with John an Okes, and John a Stiles, and with their Termes.' In other words, Nokes and Stiles were by 1650 not only surnames but legal fictions and common currency, a triple fame that their true owners must have occasionally found rather confusing—especially among the (so-called) simple rustics.

Legal again in their connexions are the coupled names Blackacre and Whiteacre, once generic for the opposing litigants; in 'The Double Dealer', that licentious but witty comedy by the Restoration dramatist, Wycherley, there is a litigious widow whose name is Mrs. Blackacre, whence, probably, arose the rare eighteenth-century verb, *blackacre*, to litigate about landed property. Landed property is the clue: in 1628, in Coke, another famous lawyer, we find *black acre* used of a specified piece of ground, to distinguish it from a second piece described as *white acre*; the latter term is recorded a little later in the same century. If perchance a third 'parcel' of ground were concerned it would be called *green acre*. As the 'Oxford English Dictionary' observes, 'the choice of the words " black ", " white " and " green " was perhaps influenced by their use to indicate different kinds of crops'. The three words have become surnames, but it is to be noted that the *acre, aker* endings are not quite so simple as they look, and of the trickiness of these names there exists no better example than *Whitaker, Whittaker*. There is a transition between *white acre* and *Whit(t)aker*: this is *witacre*. But even when we know that, we may go astray, for not only, as in the early fourteenth-century Lancashire name 'Adam de Whitekar', may the ending derive from *car* (*car* being an alder-covered marshy waste) as well as from *acre*, but the *whit(t)* may represent 'wheat' and 'wet' in addition to 'white', as I learn from Professor Ernest Weekley's 'Surnames', of which it might fairly be said that no family should be without it.

But *Blackacre* and *Whiteacre* never became typenames apart from law; they failed to achieve the distinction of *John Doe* and *Richard Roe*, *John-a-Nokes* and *Tom-a-Stiles*, which, from the sixteenth to the early nineteenth century, served occasionally in the role of what we now call *the man in the street*, a term that has replaced, but not completely ousted, *the average man*. This last, typically nineteenth century, is less interesting than *the man in the street*, of which, by the way, the American form was, until recently, *the man in the cars*, vouched for by Lord Bryce in his classic, ' The American Commonwealth ' (1888). Greville in his gossipy ' Memoirs ', at 22 March 1831, mentions that *the man in the street* is a Newmarket racing term, but it was Emerson who, in 1854, and frequently afterwards, used it in the modern sense and, by his powerful example, gave it currency ; yet it lacked a widespread popularity until some years afterwards. That it did not become familiar in Australia until the eighteen-nineties we deduce from the fact that in February 1897 Professor Edward Morris, in his ' Austral English, a Dictionary of Australasian Words, Phrases and Usages ', could write of ' the average man, whom it is the modern fashion to call " the man in the street " ' and thus afford us the pleasant experience of shooting a word on the wing. In Australia, from about ten years later, I heard *Jack Smith* employed in the same way as *the man in the street* : a usage that recalls *Brown, Jones, and Robinson*, for ' people in general '. These three names have, for England and Wales, been promoted to the place that, according to the distribution of the names concerned, belongs rightfully to *Smith, Jones, Williams*.

Somewhat different is *Tom, Dick, and Harry*, which stresses the ordinariness of the ' men taken at random from the common run '. *Tom, Dick, and Harry* did not originate until about 1815 and was for some years much more common in America than in Great Britain; as late as 1865, Alexander Smith (in his delightful 'Summer in Skye') could use a variant, *Tom, Jack, and Harry*. As early as 1596, however, Shakespeare ('or another man called Shakespeare') cites another trio, *Tom, Dick, and Francis*; he also employs *Hob* [Bob] *and Dick* in exactly the same way. Allied are *Jack and Jill*, any man and girl of 'the common people', and *Tom and Tib*, the same; connected too are *Tom Tiler*, any 'man in the street', a sixteenth to seventeenth-century term, and *Thomas* or *Tom*, any male belonging to the lower ranks of society. Such names as Tom, Dick, Harry, Frank, Jack, Bob, are made generic for the obvious reason that one could with safety address every second man by one of them; *Jack* is still very frequent among 'the common people' when, in addressing a stranger, one wishes to avoid the abruptness caused by omitting the unknown name. A much fuller list of generic Christian names is given by the poet Gower, who died in 1408: the significance of this list is to be seen by a reference to Professor Weekley's joyous 'Etymological Dictionary of Modern English'. The same authority remarks that the French say *Pierre et Paul*, the Germans *Heinz und Kunz* (Henry and Conrad).

One might 'go on for ever', but the examples given here are the principal ones; moreover, they are, in both senses, thoroughly representative.

AMERICAN CANT

TRAMPDOM AND THE UNDERWORLD

IN the December 1930 issue of 'The American Mercury', Mr. James P. Burke of Chicago gives a glossary of 'the slanguage of the racketeer'. It is an interesting vocabulary, though somewhat specialist. A very much fuller, more general and certainly no less interesting list was recently published as 'American Tramp and Underworld Slang', compiled and edited by Mr. Godfrey Irwin, an American journalist. Having spent a considerable amount of time in the company of Mr. Irwin and having passed many, many hours with his manuscript, I here sketch the main points made or implied by the author and cite a few of the 1,700 entries in his glossary. Mr. Irwin has had 'more than twenty years' experience as a tramp on the railroads, roads and tramp steamers of the United States, Canada, Mexico and Central America, and in Central American waters', and, as a 'newspaper man', he has been in very close contact with the underworld of the cities.

The slang of the American underworld and of American trampdom is grossly misunderstood by those who do not live in those very exclusive circles. Writers of fiction dealing with these two classes of society, classes that often merge, are responsible for many mistaken opinions. Even the novelists concerned with possible situations and more or less probable persons, novelists that, like Packard, Coe, and Edgar Wallace,[1] are enjoyed by the very people whom they describe, fall occasionally into error; their technical skill does not encourage them to keep strictly to the actual slang of trampdom and the underworld.

It is much rather the tramp than the criminal who propagates this slang, although it is extremely difficult, except in specific terms and phrases, to differentiate the slang of the tramp, who is 'more or less law-abiding', from that of the dyed-in-the-wool criminal. Not only do the tramps and the criminals intermix, but the army, the navy, the ordinary sailor, and the immigrant contribute largely to the capital of slangdom. Even misunderstood words and phrases add to the general stock.

But while the gangster is increasing in both power and numbers, the tramp appears to be showing the initial signs of obsolescence. The American tramps used to be chiefly those veterans of the Civil War who failed to get work or who were reluctant to return to the more humdrum joys of peace. After a while, many street urchins and youths, attracted by the picturesque 'soldiers' tales', joined the veterans. But ' forced employment during the World War, naval and military service, and the increase in criminal activities since the War have all had their part in lessening the tramp population'. There is, however, small likelihood of this slang ever becoming the general heritage of the American race.

[1] Especially in that improbable but exciting tale, ' The Northing Tramp ', which is ' laid ' in the United States.

Heritage of another kind is very marked: approximately one-quarter of the slang terms in Mr. Irwin's glossary (which I have every reason to believe to be thoroughly representative and laudably comprehensive) have parallels in current English slang or antecedents in either the thieves' cant of the sixteenth, seventeenth and eighteenth centuries or the less esoteric slang of the eighteenth and early nineteenth centuries.

But since the glossary itself is more illuminating than the numerous generalizations that one could make, a few examples may be given. The social value of such a dictionary appears from the entry at ' racket ', to take an instance almost at random. 'RACKET. Originally an entertainment or a ball, especially one given by a semi-political or a " social " club. Any " graft ", or type of criminal activity. The word was popular with the old-time safe-blowers, and is now very generally used. Doubtless its present application to the major and the minor extortions so common in the United States is due to the practice of political " heelers " or " toughs " in taking tickets for the " racket " (original sense) and forcing small shopkeepers to buy them on pain of bodily harm or destruction of their goods. The word covers every illegal or criminal activity, from the mildest and almost imperceptible blackmail to the extensive liquor- and drug-selling syndicates and the bands of blackmailers and kidnappers so frequent to-day.'

Drink and Prohibition call forth some particularly forcible comments, but most of the entries are too long for quotation. *Smoke*, which is a cheap and often poisonous liquor that, since Prohibition, has constantly been served in 'shock joints', is derived from shellac or certain other commercial alcohols or solvents, or even distilled from garbage; it is named because, when water is added, it turns cloudy if not actually smoky. We learn that some of the alternative names for intoxicant liquor are *rot-gut, alki, lush, third rail*.

The drug-taking so prevalent in the United States since the introduction of Prohibition is responsible for many of the terms in recent and current slang. A *junker* is the usual name of a drug-addict, though *dope-fiend* is the more common in ordinary 'respectable' slang; in the underworld, the other terms most frequently used are *dope, junk hound, hypo,* and *snow bird*. *Junker* comes, obviously, from *junk*, which, we learn, has, from the normal meaning of 'anything worthless', been restricted to narcotic drugs: cocaine, opium, and their derivatives yen shee, morphine, heroin, laudanum, paregoric. The note that follows is so significant that I feel bound to quote it in full: 'Morphine, a derivative of opium, is the drug most commonly used, although cocaine is also popular with a great number of addicts, as is heroin, an acetyl derivative of morphine. This last is an anodyne and a sedative when properly administered, as well as the most powerful of habit-forming drugs: it is this which causes so much of the crime in America to-day, the addict not only stealing and killing to obtain the money necessary to purchase his drug, but losing much of his native sense and caution when under the spell of the drug or when desperately in need of a dose or " shot ". Opium itself is no longer used so commonly as before, since it requires an elaborate and often expensive smoking-outfit as well as a secluded room where doors and windows may be sealed to prevent the escape of the tell-tale odour.'

Of the terms associated especially with the underworld, *stool*, *squealer*, *frame-up*, and *on the spot* are familiar to most readers of modern fiction. Yet, despite the popularity of Edgar Wallace's play, how many persons really do know the full connotation of *on the spot*? It was originally a railway phrase indicating a truck or van set on a side track or alongside a platform: 'spotted' there for loading or unloading. The underworld adopted it. Thus a person is placed 'on the spot' when he is lured to any given place that he might there be shot or bombed to death, or when he is 'framed' by his former confederates or accomplices so that he is convicted of a capital crime, or, again, when he is deliberately endangered in some other and expectedly-fatal way. In brief, then, the phrase means 'in danger' or 'marked-down to be murdered'.

The criminal of trampdom is the *yegg*. At first this word designated any man too old or cowardly, too cautious or too wise, to risk crime in the cities; hence, a tramp thief. The *tramp* proper is he who 'wanders but never works'. The *hobo* belongs to the race, but not to the fraternity, of tramps; the *bum* is also only a near-tramp, for he does not 'tramp' any more than he can help. Mr. Irwin, without disclosing the identity of this evidently-knowledgeable fellow, says that, according to 'an experienced hobo', the difference is this: 'Bums loafs and sits. Tramps loafs and walks. But a hobo moves and works—and he's clean!' The periodic camps of tramps and hoboes are known as *jungles*, their favourite food is *mulligan*, a stew of varying ingredients with a meat-base.

Certain words are entertaining, but not, like those just mentioned, so much for their social connotations as for their precise denotations or for their etymology. Among the former are *clean*, which means out of funds, penniless; i.e. free or clean of that which defiles, ' filthy lucre ', but perhaps merely an American contraction of *clean broke*. *Lace curtains* are long and voluminous whiskers, sometimes called *wind-tormentors*. We have all heard, perhaps too often heard, of *necking*, which, however, means in the underworld no more than to stare at, to watch closely, the word coming from *rubber neck*, that priceless Americanism for one so inquisitive that he stares until his neck is stretched.

A quaint etymological interest attaches to numerous words in the vocabulary of the American tramps and criminals; the following may serve as specimens.[1] *Limey* is an Englishman: in the days before steam, the English ships served out lime-juice to prevent scurvy; at that time, the term was used in profound scorn by the envious American sailors; now it is a perfectly neutral word. A *magazine* is a six months' imprisonment, this being the time required by one of the unlettered to read this type of periodical. *To pineapple* is to bomb or to dynamite, from the *pineapple* (a bomb) so much used by gangster, extortioner, and the police; the word was brought from France by the American soldiers, who took it over from the Tommy. A *shave-tail* was originally a mule; mules newly received into the Army had their tails cropped; the term was seized by the ribald ' ranker ' to designate a second lieutenant; since the War, *shave-tail*

[1] Irwin's book is published by the Oxford University Press at 10*s*. 6*d*. net.

denotes one who, none too capable, is yet anxious to exercise his authority. A *meestle* is a dog; 'taken from the Gypsy', says Mr. Irwin, 'and very old indeed, though seldom heard among the younger tramps and criminals'. It is probably a corruption of either *messan* (as in Robert Burns) or *messet* (a provincial form of the same word), or a confusion of both; the original meaning was lap-dog, and as used by Burns, Scott, and several other writers it does indeed imply some connexion with Gypsies. *Jerry* has been adopted from Cockney slang. Signifying to suspect or to perceive, a trick or deception, it is a synonym of *rumble* and *tumble* (or *tumble to*), and the key is perhaps this: in Cockney rhyming slang, 'to tumble' was expressed by *jerrycummumble* or *Jerry the humble*, and (as *China*, a mate, a pal, is short for *China plate*) the rhyming-slang term was shortened to *jerry*. In the lowest slang, in fact, there are many curious developments such as that of *China* and *jerry*; subtlety occasionally crops up in a very odd form.

THE WORD BLOODY

Among tragic downfalls from high to the lowest place, the unfortunate and familiar adjectives *blooming* and *bloody* are deserving of sympathetic mention.

LOGAN PEARSALL SMITH

IN his 'social pity' novel 'All Sorts and Conditions of Men'—one of the best that he wrote after his collaborator Rice's death in 1882—Besant has this illuminating passage: 'The man replied that he did not know the object of the building; and to make quite manifest that he really did not know, he put an adjective before the word "object", and another—that is, the same—before the word "building". With that he passed on his way, and Lord Jocelyn was left marvelling at the slender resources of our language, which makes one adjective do duty for so many qualifications.' Commenting on this, Professor Weekley [1] has compared the British workman's exclusive preference for *bloody* with the refined circles' *nice*, the schoolgirls' *ripping*, and the schoolboys' *decent*.

Much the same point of view has been expressed by Professor Wyld,[2] who treats also of a further aspect

---

[1] 'The Romance of Names', 1914. I use the carefully revised edition of 1928.

[2] 'A History of Colloquial English', 1920.

of great significance. 'There is a certain adjective, most offensive to polite ears,'—the Professor avoids mentioning it by name and excludes it from both the indexes in the book from which I quote—' which plays apparently the chief role in the vocabulary of large sections of the community. It seems to argue a certain poverty of linguistic resource when we find that this word is used by the same speakers both to mean absolutely nothing—being placed before every noun, and often adverbially before . . . adjectives— and also to mean a great deal—everything indeed that is unpleasant in the highest degree. It is rather a curious fact that the word in question while always impossible, except perhaps when used as it were in inverted commas, in such a way that the speaker dissociates himself from all responsibility for, or proprietorship in it, would be felt to be rather more than ordinarily intolerable, if it were used by an otherwise polite speaker as an absolutely meaningless adjective prefixed at random to most of the nouns in a sentence, and worse than if it were used deliberately, with a settled and full intent. There is something very terrible in an oath torn from its proper home and suddenly implanted in the wrong social atmosphere. In these circumstances the alien form is endowed by the hearers with mysterious and uncanny meanings; it chills the blood and raises gooseflesh.' But *bloody* no longer chills the blood: it is frequently employed to warm the conversation, and it has become one of the tricks of the best-selling—and other—novelists. The Professor's statement, however, accounts for the sensation caused by George Bernard Shaw's employment of the word two years before the War.

THE WORD BLOODY

The O.E.D. dates the low English usage of *bloody*, 'an epithet expressing detestation' when not merely an intensive (especially in the negative, e.g. 'not a bloody one'), from about 1840, and surmises that this sense of *bloody* derives from that of the adverb, which, in good and general colloquial use and odour until about 1750, became popular during the Restoration in its present form: Etherege in his comedy 'The Man of Mode', 1676, has 'not without he will promise to be bloody drunk', the phrase *bloody drunk* recurring in Dryden. Professor Weekley has, in his 'Words Ancient and Modern', shown that *bloody* for *bloodily* 'is due to an instinct which tends to drop *-ly* from a word already ending in *-y*', as in *very*, *pretty*, *jolly* : 'Mr. Masefield's beautiful line, "I'll bloody burn his bloody ricks", would lose all its rhythm and much of its charm, if the correct adverb were substituted before "burn"'. (I would like to record my belief that in 'The Everlasting Mercy', 1912,— a 'dramatic poem' sensational for its bad language, —Mr. Masefield was wrong to use *bloody* thus before *burn* : such a character[1] would have said 'bloody well burn'.)

Professor Weekley adduces a most helpful earlier example from John Marston's 'Faun', 1606 : there someone is described as 'cruelly eloquent and bluddily learned'. *Bloodily* as an intensive adverb probably came in with the Elizabethans, and I shall be surprised if research does not reveal that one of the pamphleteers introduced it. The Restoration writers employed the adverbial *bloody* without offence, and in the first half of the eighteenth century it was quite respectable,

[1] See the song 'Raining', quoted later.

as we see from the following three examples.[1] Swift in 1714 writes to Stella, 'It was bloody hot walking to-day'; in 1727 in one of his works the Dean has 'His wife ... said, "Are you not sick, my dear?" He replied, "Bloody sick"'; and in 1742 Samuel Richardson, blameless to the point of goody-goodyness, says of a character in Pamela, 'He is bloody passionate.' In 1753 Samuel Foote, the actor-dramatist, has what has become a stock phrase, 'She's a bloody fine girl,' which represents the transition from respectability to indecency. Thereafter the adverb was increasingly banned, and not until the 1840's [2] did the adjective become at all common with workmen and their social equals, whose privilege it remained until Masefield, Shaw, and the War foisted it on the public. The public, it may be remarked, has since 1912 done all the publicity needed to introduce it into every class.

It is worth noting that in the revised Hotten of 1874 stands this significant entry:[3] 'BLOODY, an expletive word, without reference to meaning as an adjective and an adverb, simply for intensification.' In 1880 Ruskin alluded to its use, 'not altering the form of the word, but defiling the thought in it'. Ten years later, John S. Farmer said of the adjective that while it has many 'vague and varying senses', it usually has no meaning; occasionally it 'carries with it a suspicion of anger, resentment, or detestation'. The same applies to the adverb, as Wright has made quite clear in 1897.

[1] From the O.E.D. and Weekley's 'Etymological Dictionary'.
[2] Dana, 'Before the Mast', 1840, has 'You'll find me a bloody rascal.'
[3] Its significance is ignored by the standard lexicographers.

THE WORD BLOODY

Going back ten years, we see that Charles Mackay, in his article ' English Slang and French Argot ' in ' Blackwood's Magazine ' for May 1888, speaks of ' such shallow semblances of the broader oaths of a bygone age as " darn " for " damn ", " so help me Scott " for " so help me God ", and " blooming " for " bloody " ' ; he notes that *bloody* is much more generally used in England than in America and—this, I must remind you, is in 1888—' seldom long absent from the conversation of the vilest classes of low Englishman '. The word does not escape that Irish-Gaelic mania which Mackay displayed in his writings on words (he even combed Littré's famous dictionary to impose Celtic roots on to a multitude of innocent French words) : *bloody*, he says, ' is not really synonymous with sanguinary in its etymological origin, though it is usually held to be so, but proceeds from a British root of quite a different and altogether inoffensive meaning—from *bloidhe*, " rather " ; as when Dean Swift wrote to a friend in England that it was " bloody hot in Dublin ", he simply meant in Irish-Gaelic phrase that it was rather hot.' Mackay then sagely remarks : ' But the English lower classes, who employ the word so frequently, though they sometimes substitute " blooming ", would not perhaps interlard their talk with it so persistently and offensively if they knew that no greater force attached to it than . . . " rather " '. No, they wouldn't and they don't. It is precisely these classes which have the alternative *bleeding*,[1] and even *bleed*[2] for blood as in ' I'll have

---

[1] Wright in ' The English Dialect Dictionary ' records *bleedy* (or *bleady*) as an adverb. *Bleeding* is both adverb and adjective.
[2] Now obsolescent.

his bleed '; *bleeder*, for an adjectival chap, was often employed in 1914–18 by the Tommy and is of Cockney origin. *Blooming* is equally a corruption with *blurry*, which as used in newspapers and books during the War was an euphemism, but as used in actual speech is merely a slurring of the original. Likewise, *blinking* is not directly an euphemism for *bloody* : it probably represents *blanking*, i.e. *bleeding*, i.e. *bloody*, as in ' the blinking thing ', and the relationship is more clearly seen in *blinker*, pejorative for chap, fellow, man, and very closely resembling *bleeder*.

The difference between the English and the American attitude was again mentioned in 1893, when to ' Harper's Magazine ' (nearly as good then as it is now—we still have nothing like it in England) Professor J. Brander Matthews contributed a revolutionary essay,[1] somewhat influenced it is true by Lounsbury, on ' The Function of Slang '. There he reinforces Mackay on one point : ' Every American traveler in England must have remarked with surprise the British use of the Saxon synonym of *sanguinary* as an intensive, the chief British rivals of *bloody* in this respect being *blooming* and *blasted*. All these are held to be shocking to polite ears, and it was with bated breath that the editor of a London newspaper wrote about the prospects of " a b——y war " ; while, as another London editor declared recently, it is now impossible for a cockney to read with proper sympathy Jeffrey's appeal to Carlyle, after a visit to Craigenputtock, to bring his " blooming Eve out of her blasted para-

[1] Reprinted in the volume entitled ' Parts of Speech ', a most interesting collection of essays and studies on language—English and American.

THE WORD BLOODY

dise ".' And Mr. Mencken [1] has judiciously recorded that *bloody* ' is entirely without improper significance in America '.

In the present century, the use of both adjective and adverb has spread in every direction.

It was in 1912 that George Bernard Shaw startled London and, indeed, fluttered the whole Empire by making one of the characters in ' Pygmalion ' use the word in ordinary dialogue. In Act III, where Liza Dolittle is being ' inspected ' by Higgins's relatives and friends, that young flower-girl from Covent Garden, when Freddy, opening the door for her, asks : ' Are you walking across the Park, Miss Dolittle ? If so——', replies : ' Walk ! Not bloody likely. (*Sensation.*) I am going in a taxi.' Much of the interest felt in the play was due to ' the heroine's utterance of this banned word. It was waited for with trembling, heard shudderingly. . . .' [2] Referring to the year 1910, C. E. Montague made one of the characters in ' Rough Justice ' (1926) declare very acutely : ' All the little different emphasizing particles in Greek mean what an English workman means by bloody.' That would be equally true of the British soldier in 1914–18 when language was callously, cynically, mockingly, or desperately and sadistically, debased : when, with a supreme disregard to discrimination, the troops could, as W. V. Tilsley in ' Other Ranks ', 1931, remarked, say that ' Snow was bloody, khaki was bloody, the sky was bloody, green envelopes were bloody '. Compare their song ' Raining ' (to the

[1] H. L. Mencken, ' The American Language ', 3rd edition, 1923 (1st, 1919).
[2] ' The (New York) Times ', April 14, 1914.

air of the hymn 'Holy, Holy, Holy'), which begins :

> Raining, raining, raining,
> Always bloodywell raining.
> Raining all the morning,
> And raining all the night,

and ends

> Marching, marching, marching,
> Always bloodywell marching ;
> When the war is over
> We'll bloodywell march no more.[1]

Bloody was their favourite adverb and adjective : all other ' swear words ', frequently as some were used, might be described as ' also-rans '. It even served as an intersyllabic or intervocalic word, as in ' im-bloody-possible ' or ' too bloody right '.

In 1919 Mr. H. L. Mencken could assert that ' so familiar has it become . . . that it is a mere counter-word, without intelligible significance ', and he illustrated this with the story, current since the late nineteenth century, of two Yorkshiremen in front of an election poster. ' What do they mean ', asks one, ' by one man, one vote ? ' ' Why ! ' answered his companion, ' it means " one bloody man, one bloody vote ",' to which the inquirer replied, ' Then why the hell don't they bloody well say so ? ' A decade later, the Very Rev. Dean Inge observed that in the speech of the British workman, *bloody* served merely to indicate that a noun or an adjective might be expected to follow immediately. In its origin, however, the

---

[1] From John Brophy : ' Songs and Slang of the British Soldier ', 3rd edition, 1931.

word was perhaps due [1] to the 'instinct for adorning every object'; 'like other more or less useless things the adjective is merely used as packing material'.

The origin is somewhat doubtful and, as Mencken has remarked, 'just why it is regarded as profane and indecent by the English is one of the mysteries of the language'. The proposed etymologies number six.

1. Charles Mackay's *bloidhe*, rather. Already mentioned, this fantastic suggestion merits no further attention.

2. *By'r Lady* [2] (originally *by our Lady*), 'an interjection very common in Shakespeare, in no way corresponding in use to *bloody*'. Even in the oft-cited instance in Swift, 'it grows by'r Lady cold', the oath is obviously an oath; like all oaths, it is used for emphasis, but that doesn't make it an adverb, still less the adverb *bloody*. This delusion 'seems ineradicable'.

3. *S'blood* (originally *God's blood*), another ancient oath. As improbable as No. 2.

4. *Blood* in its ordinary physiological sense but with reference to either menstruation (as noted by Mencken) or 'the bloody flux', the old name for dysentery. Ingenious, but the explanation is much too restricted to be valid.

5. *A blood*, a rich (and generally young) roisterer. Of *bloody* the O.E.D. says: 'There is good reason to think that it was at first a reference to the habits of the " bloods " or aristocratic rowdies of the end of the seventeenth and beginning of the eighteenth century. The phrase " bloody drunk " was apparently

[1] Weekley, 'Adjectives and Other Words', 1930.
[2] Mostly from Weekley's 'Words Ancient and Modern', 1926.

= " as drunk as a blood " (cf. " as drunk as a lord "); thence it was extended to kindred expressions, and at length to others.' It is interesting to note that Grose records the phrase 'drunk as an emperor', i.e. ten times as drunk as a lord, but it does not materially affect the argument, which has been changed considerably by Weekley's example of 1606, which disposes pretty thoroughly of the 'aristocratic roisterer' theory.

6. *Blood* as physiological blood in general. In 'a man cruelly eloquent and bluddily learned', *cruelly* may retain something of the sense 'severely', 'distressingly', but this adverb early became an intensive meaning little more than 'very' as in 'cruelly cold'; likewise *bluddily*, as it is there spelt, may preserve some connotation of 'vividly', 'spiritedly', 'heatedly' or 'enthusiastically'. But, all in all, both words connote little more than 'exceedingly'. It is, however, noticeable that the root-idea of blood as something vivid or distressing or both still colours the use of the adjective, which is, as it has always been, stronger and less 'polite' than the adverb: but then adverbs in general lose their original signification more rapidly than adjectives in general do theirs. There is no doubt that *bloody* has been chosen as an expletive 'for its grisly and repellent sound and sense' and that its frequent association with battle, murder, wounds, outrage, insult and kindred facts has strengthened its appeal to those who like a violent word: at first, these were the rougher members of the lower classes. Its use is similar to that of *terrible, devilish, damned, beastly, filthy*, and their adverbs.

The corresponding word is similarly employed in

other languages. The Latin adjective *cruentus* is found not only with *victoria*, *pax*, *bellum*, but with *ira* and *dies*, and, more significantly still, the adverb *cruente(r)* sometimes, in post-Augustan Latin, means nothing more than 'severely'. In Greek we find αἱματόεις πόλεμος, a bloody war. Professor Weekley shows that the modern languages offer further parallels. He cites instances from the Dutch, French, German, and gives two particularly valuable ones from the second: 'Voltaire, in his "Commentaire sur Corneille", writes, "La princesse Henriette joua un tour bien sanglant (a bloody trick) à Corneille, quand elle le fit travailler à Bérénice", and the word is still used with *injure*, *reproche*, *outrage*, &c. If we go still further back, we find, in a fourteenth-century report of a marital dispute, that "elle l'appela sanglant sourd et lui l'appela sanglante ordure".' The Dutch equivalent of *une sanglante injure* (a bloody insult) is *een bloedige beleediging* or *een bloedige hoon*. The German *blutig* (in compounds *blut*) can, in certain senses, exactly render the English *bloody* as in 'Ich habe keinen blutigen Heller mehr', I haven't a bloody bean, or, less slangily, I have not even a penny left; *blutarm*, miserably or bloody poor; the archaic *blutdieb* signifies a bloody thief; while 'Das ist mein blutiger Ernst' is, as Professor Weekley says, 'fairly polite German for ' I seriously (Shavian *bloodywell*) mean what I say "'.

The sixth, the physiologico-affective etymology and explanation, is the natural one, and really there was never any need to be tortuously or pedantically ingenious.

It is in some ways a pity that *bloody* has been thus

debased, despite the vigour of its expletive use, for the debasement has been so general that, in serious contexts, we are now, in order to avoid a titter, forced to use severe, cruel or sanguinary instead of an excellent word.

EUPHEMISM AND EUPHEMISMS

Substitution of mild or vague expression for harsh or blunt one; expression thus substituted.
H. W. AND F. G. FOWLER

OF the numerous writers who have dealt with this subject, I shall take an assortment chosen for their different nationalities and their varying points of view: an Englishman, an American, an Italian, a Frenchman, and a Belgian. They all assume that we know the etymology of the word, which derives from a Greek verb meaning 'to speak favourably'. Greek provides what is perhaps the most famous of all euphemisms: *Eumenides*, the Kindly Ones, for the Furies or Avenging Gods.

Professor Weekley, in 'The Romance of Words', speaks of euphemism as 'that form of speech which avoids calling things by their names' and observes that it results from 'various human instincts which range from religious reverence down to common decency' and, he implies, a good deal lower. He cites two interesting examples of that modesty which leads to much euphemism: 'In 1829 the use of the word *mouchoir*', a handkerchief, 'in a French adaptation of "Othello" caused a riot at the Comédie Française. History repeats itself, for, in 1907, a play by J. M. Synge was produced in Dublin, but "the audience broke up in disorder at the word *shift*".'

Handkerchief itself is a euphemism, with the ludicrous literal meaning of hand-cover-head, while *shift* is an earlier euphemism (literally, a change of raiment) for a smock.

Among Americans, Greenough and Kittredge in ' Words and Their Ways in English Speech ', Mr. H. L. Mencken in ' The American Language ', and Professor George McKnight in ' English Words and Their Background ' have written both thoughtfully and entertainingly on the subject : where so much is good, the last will serve. McKnight stresses the fact that the Greeks and many other races believed—many people still do believe—that ' there is a direct relation between a thing and its name ' : this belief links intimately with religious and other superstition, of which more anon. He points out that, contrary to a rather general impression, ' one of the most distinctive features of sophisticated speech, as distinguished from unsophisticated speech in our time '—his book appeared in 1923—' is the absence of squeamishness and the ready courage to name things directly ' : since the War, in fact, it is only the semi-educated and the uneducated who have persisted in consistent euphemism, and, since civilization began, it has always been the ' half-baked ' who practise euphemism the most.

The Italian selected is Niceforo,[1] who relates all ancient euphemism to superstition of some kind or other and implies that a modern sincerely disclaiming such an origin and alleging modesty or respect or kindness is nevertheless traditionalist ; that, in other words, he unthinkingly preserves what was once either

[1] Alfredo Niceforo : ' Le Génie de l'Argot ', 1912. His early books were written in his native language, his later in French.

pure superstition or a social usage based on superstition. The Frenchman is M. Henri Bauche, author of that somewhat technical but interesting work, ' Le Langage Populaire ' (1920). He has contributed to the subject chiefly by pointing out that the distinction between the harsh or the gross word and that which is not considered such is somewhat arbitrary in all languages, that the harshness or the grossness does not correspond exactly to the picture evoked by the word, that different peoples and different social classes vary considerably not only at different but at the same periods with regard to what things, as well as what words, are to be regarded as objectionable, and that in one restricted but significant group (that of physical intimacy and the sexual parts) the euphemisms are due to the fact that the anatomical terms would be both misplaced and pompously ridiculous, while the ' old Roman words ' have become too gross to be used by the respectable.

Professor Carnoy, of the University of Louvain, in an even more technical and even more interesting work, ' La Science du Mot ' (1927), has a very important chapter on euphemism and its opposite, dysphemism. Euphemism he neatly defines as discretion, which does, after all, account for almost every example of euphemism—if we consider discretion in its widest sense. He shrewdly notes that euphemism is employed not to hide the truth or the fact or the thing (silence is best for that) but merely to minimize the painful impression on the listener or the unpleasant results for the speaker, this latter aspect having never been adequately treated until Carnoy took it in hand ; related to this latter is the speaker's desire to make a favourable impression. All this appears in the Professor's classification of the direct causes of euphemism and the particular reasons for its use, a classification that I cannot forbear reproducing, though I modify it somewhat.

1. *The desire to adapt oneself to the general sentiment suitable to the time, place, and other circumstances.* This desire will take one of two forms : Carnoy notes only the anxiety not to depart from an elevated or a beautiful style in poetry, oratory, &c., by introducing unseemly or trivial words or metaphors. But in very lowly or very friendly circles, or in addressing children, one may try to avoid technical or literary words by employing synonyms that are definitely euphemistic ; in conversation with children, of course, a euphemism is frequently due to a modesty that would be wholly out of place between adults or to a wish to spare children knowledge that might, to them, be either painful or meaningless.

2. *The effort to enhance the value of what one possesses or of what one gives.* This is hyperbole, and the relation of hyperbole to euphemism is nowhere so well treated as in McKnight's book already mentioned. As in *saloon* for a bar, *university* for a technical school, *professor* for a teacher or simply an exponent.

3. *Respect for the person addressed, or the desire to impress or please the person addressed.* Under this heading come titles, the stereotyped politeness of the professions and of commerce, the calling of a Jew a *Hebrew*,[1] a negro

---

[1] This is a particularly glaring example, for no decent Jew wants to be called anything else : why on earth should he ! for he has nothing of which to be ashamed and much to make him proud of his race.

a *coloured man* (even *gentleman*), any woman a *lady*. Some of the most ridiculous of euphemisms are due to this desire and this practice; it is, however, to be noticed that such instances of euphemism result not from a desire to impress or to please but from an often mistaken reluctance to offend either the person addressed, or perhaps somebody within hearing, as in the ridiculous *dark gentleman* for an Indian of India and in *charlady* for a charwoman. If one is speaking to a person less directly concerned, the avoidance links up with the next group.

4. *The need to diminish, to tone down a painful evocation, to soften tragic news.* That, among civilized peoples and especially in refined circles, is the most frequent of all reasons. Death above all, but also sickness, madness or idiocy, ruin. *To pass away, be no more, leave this world, be asleep in the Lord, expire, to go west*, and many other terms instead of the simple ' to die ', and this tendency has spread to undertakers and their functions: *funeral director, obsequies*, and other atrocities.

5. *Social and Moral Taboos.* In every class, there are actions and objects that are blameworthy or very intimate and therefore not mentioned directly in good company. A mild example is drunkenness, which prompts all sorts of euphemisms: *half seas over, elevated, lively, a bit on, happy*. The ' inferior ' physical processes and functions afford a stronger and better example, and for these delicacy, reticence, and politeness devise euphemisms as discreet as *to retire* or *pay a visit*. All that relates to sex is heavily veiled: a pregnant woman is *in an interesting condition*; a person lacking in restraint is *fast*; a mistress is a *friend*;

the intimacy of marriage becomes *conjugal relations*; obscene becomes *blue* or *hot* or even *frank*.

6. *Superstitious Taboos and Religious Interdictions.* The word is God; speech has a mysterious power; the name evokes the thing. These three points of view explain many ancient and modern euphemisms, and the same emotion or attitude, at different stages, is represented by the philosophic concept of the *Logos* and the popular belief implicit in *speak of the devil*. The latter is seen in the old superstition that one must be particularly careful how one speaks of God, the gods, important persons, the dead; especially with regard to the Deity, this belief survives in such terms as *by golly!*, *by gad!*, *gee-whiz!*, the *deuce!* Superstition may, however, become pure reverence, and reverence of another kind is felt by those truly in love, to whom it dictates a euphemistic vocabulary of intimacy.

These six reasons could be reduced to three: fear, kindness, delicacy, as anyone can see if he examines a list of euphemisms. That point need not be laboured, but in euphemism and euphemisms there are certain important features that cannot be ignored.

The need for euphemism is one of the chief causes of synonyms, though it is far from being the only one. Any very general act—to eat, to walk, to sleep—has a rich synonymy; so has any very usual object—a head, a hand, a house. But when, further, that act or object or condition is not considered respectable or if it is very intimate, then the synonymy becomes richer still. The need—sometimes real, sometimes imagined —for euphemism has led to much verbal ingenuity, rarely beautiful, often clever, occasionally morbid.

Euphemism may cause the word it replaces to be forgotten or to become obsolete. Frequently it causes successive synonyms to be suspect, displeasing, indelicate, immoral, or blasphemous. This we see in such words as *lover* and *mistress*, *simple* and *silly*, and, in certain contexts, *weak* and *strong*, while an excellent example in French is *fille*. As Weekley has said, ' a euphemism is doomed from its very birth ', and as Carnoy has expatiated : ' la vertu adoucissante des termes euphémistiques n'est naturellement pas de très longue durée. Dès que les gens se sont pour de bon habitués à comprendre B quand on dit A, A exprime aussi clairement B que le symbole propre à ce dernier. Il faut donc recommencer et aller chercher un nouveau mot qui puisse voiler B sans l'obscurcir tout à fait. Dans l'entretemps, A s'est définitivement infecté du sens défavorable de B et s'est donc *dégradé*.'

Euphemism may be obtained by directing the thought in the desired direction as in *honorarium*, *convey* (to steal), *spend the night with*, by using an extremely vague phrase as in *she made a slip*, by mentioning a significantly concomitant circumstance as in *remove* (to kill), by being enigmatical or elusive as in *lose the number of one's mess* (to die), by understatement and the negative litotes as in *have a glass* (to become drunk), *it's not too good*, by irony, by employing another language, by reticence as in *you know where to go*, i.e. go to hell !, and by abbreviation as in *w.c.* and *T.B.* (more properly *Tb*).

It was in the nineteenth century that euphemism in England and America reached its height. It had gradually increased from the time of the French Revolution until about 1835, and at that pitch it remained for some forty years ; nor did the freedom comparable with that of the eighteenth century reappear until the War. We have not yet returned to the absence of euphemism that characterized the Restoration and the late Elizabethan and early Jacobean days : there are few to desire such a return.

All in all, as Mencken observes, ' the Englishman . . . is more plain-spoken than the American, and such terms as *bitch, mare* and *in foal* do not commonly daunt him, largely, perhaps, because of his greater familiarity with country life. . . . The Victorian era saw a great growth of absurd euphemisms in England, but it was in America that the thing was carried farthest. Bartlett [1] hints that *rooster* came into use in place of *cock* as a matter of delicacy, the latter word having acquired an indecent anatomical significance, and tells us that . . . even *bull* was banned as too vulgar for refined ears '. (One shudders to think of the repressed dirtiness of mind implicit in these substitutions.) ' In place of it the early purists used *cow-creature, male-cow* and even *gentleman-cow. Bitch, ram, boar, stallion, buck,* and *sow* went the same way Bache [2] tells us that *pismire* was also banned, *antmire* being substituted for it. *To castrate* became *to alter*. In 1847 the word *chair* was actually barred out and *seat* adopted in its place. Those were the palmy days of euphemism,' when table-legs were draped ! Women, who became *females*, were shielded from anything resembling evil : one authority informs us that to

[1] In his ' Dictionary of Americanisms ', 1848 ; revised edition, 1859.
[2] Richard Bache : ' Vulgarisms and Other Errors of Speech ', 2nd edition, 1869.

mention the word *shirt* in her presence was to insult her; another that *corset* was banned; a third that '*decent* was indecent in the South: no respectable woman was supposed to have any notion of the difference between *decent* and *indecent*'. It was at this period that a wife became *lady*, a leg *limb*, a breast *bosom*,[1] while *stomach*, as Mencken caustically notes, ' was transformed, by some unfathomable magic, into a euphemism denoting the whole region from the nipples to the pelvic arch '.

The parts of the body, indeed, have suffered gravely from this false modesty; the good English word *belly* is still called stomach; and other instances have just been cited. Moreover, the lewd-minded persons of refinement transferred this abhorrence of anything so unseemly as legs (male or female), belly (likewise), buttocks (likewise), and breast (especially the female breasts) to the garments that lay next to them. For *smock*, as we have seen, *shift* was substituted; when *shift* became indelicate, the French *chemise* was adopted. *Drawers* (women's) became *knickers* or *panties*, and chemise and knickers, considered together, are often termed *lingerie* or *undies* (in 1933 slang, *scanties*) instead of underclothes or underwear: in 1900, apparently, the term was *flannels* or *linen*. So with men: *shirt*, before ladies, was banned; *breeches* became smallclothes or knickerbockers. The male trousers, indeed,

[1] Weekley, in ' The Romance of Words ', quotes from Marryat's ' Peter Simple ' (early eighteen-thirties) : ' Fate had placed me opposite to a fine turkey. I asked my partner if I should have the pleasure of helping her to a piece of the breast. She looked at me indignantly and said, " Curse your impudence, sar ; I wonder where you larn manners. Sar, I take a lilly turkey *bosom*, if you please." '

had generated a droll synonymy. *Irrepressibles* is the earliest of the genteel euphemisms for breeches (properly coming to just below the knee) or trousers (full length) : it dates from 1790. It was shortly followed by *indescribables*, 1794 ; thirty years later came *ineffables*. In the 'thirties arose *unmentionables*, used in America before being brought to England by Dickens, who in the same year (1836) coined *inexplicables* ; and, a year later, *unwhisperables*. During 1840–3 three other euphemisms were coined : *innominables, indispensables*, and *unutterables*. Of these,[1] the two that have worn best are *inexpressibles* and, above all, *unmentionables*.

Death, madness, suicide, hanging, prostitution, all have numerous synonyms, mostly euphemisms. Death has already been considered, suicide and hanging we will omit as being rather too grim. Disease of any kind—the word *disease*, literally discomfort, is itself a euphemism—is nearly always glossed over, especially if it be mental. *Mad* became *crazy*, which became *insane*, which became *lunatic*, which became *(mentally) deranged* ; *crazy* is now almost as harsh as *mad* and is more harsh than *lunatic* or *insane* ; but all these terms have had a long life. Slangy and colloquial euphemisms are *(to have) apartments to let, a screw loose, bats in one's belfry, a tile loose, a bee in one's bonnet*, and *(to be) batty, cracked, crackers, dippy, dotty, barmy, loony, strange* or *queer, touched, scatty, not all there, wrong in one's head, off one's rocker* (more usually in the form *go off one's rocker*), *off one's chump* or *head* : slang, it will be observed, is not quite so sensitive on the subject as standard English, but it is rarely cruel. In Victorian

---

[1] The terms I have collected from Hotten and from Farmer and Henley ; the dates from the O.E.D.

days, prostitution was banned as a theme, and 'to this day', wrote Mencken in 1923, 'the effects of that old reign of terror' (the Comstock Postal Act of precisely fifty years earlier) 'are still with us. We yet use . . . such idiotic forms as *red-light district, disorderly house, social disease* and *white slave*. . . . The vice crusaders, if they have accomplished nothing else, have at least forced many of the newspapers to use the honest terms, *syphilis, prostitute* and *venereal disease*'. That holds rather more of the United States than of England, but it is true of both. Since the War, however, it has been becoming yearly more permissible to speak of *brothel, prostitute, procurer, pimp* and *syphilis*, not that they are ever likely, in Britain or America, to be made general subjects of conversation! The euphemisms for a prostitute are illuminating, and I leave it to my readers to seek the full details in Wyld's 'Universal Dictionary', or in the 'Shorter Oxford Dictionary'. Here are a few: *anonyma, incognita,* and the obsolete *quaedam* ; *lady of easy virtue* or *accommodating morals* or *more complaisance than virtue* ; *sister of the night* and *street-walker* ; *courtesan* ; *Columbine* ; *gay woman* and *pretty lady* and *perfect lady* ; an *unfortunate*. This last is very frequent and Hotten remarks that while Tom Hood used the term 'in its widest and more general sense', this 'modern euphemism' derived from his famous poem 'The Bridge of Sighs':

> One more unfortunate,
> Weary of breath,
> Rashly importunate,
> Gone to her death.

Looking back, I conclude that while it is weak-minded to employ a euphemism for drunkenness, madness, disease, death (and its analogues), and prostitution, it is a lack of either tact or kindness to force these subjects on those who feel a genuine shrinking, not merely a guilty or sadistic thrill at their mention ; that sexual intimacy is all the better for being respected ; that religious matters require no euphemisms ; that euphemisms for garments are ridiculous, as are those for non-sexual parts of the body ; that perversion is so distasteful to the normal that they naturally avoid talking of it and, if forced to discuss it, are laudably reticent.

II

SEMI-BIOGRAPHICAL

ONE OF JOHN WESLEY'S SIDE-LINES

JOHN WESLEY, born at Epworth in 1703 and dying in 1791, may—despite his brother Charles's claim—be said to have originated Methodism in 1729 at Oxford, where he was for some years a Classical don. Methodism proper began in the late seventeen-thirties and until 1744 its course was determined more or less by circumstance. Although, from 1740 until his death, Wesley was immersed in his missionary and administrative work, he yet found time to write—not wholly on Methodism; perhaps, in his conscientious way, he wished to employ all his faculties; and that his education was excellent and his faculties remarkable has been too little recognized—a defect that is, however, remedied by the soundest and most entertaining of all his biographers, Mr. C. E. Vulliamy, who thus admirably summarizes the great Methodist's role and influence: 'He had done much to prepare England for the shock of the French Revolution. It is not too much to say that he was a chief agent in the stabilization of the national temper at a critical period.' 'We cannot', he continues, 'give John Wesley a place among the great intellectual reformers of the Church; we cannot set him by the side of Wycliff or Luther, Calvin or Melanchthon. But if we place what is purely spiritual above what is purely intellectual, if the elevation of philosophy is yet below the elevation of saintliness, then we can surely place him in the highest company of all. " I do indeed live by preaching," he said. He was a great light, rising in a time of darkness and confusion, and showing men that a vital religion was the one thing which could give them happiness and security and peace.'

He was also a man of exceptional energy and endurance, of great personal charm, good humour and not a little wit, kindly and thoughtful and upright. All these qualities appear even in his Dictionary. The first edition came out late in 1753; it was published at Bristol, as was the second edition early in 1764. To 'The Complete English Dictionary, Explaining most of those Hard Words, Which are found in the Best British Writers. By a Lover of Good English and Common Sense', he added, on the title-page, these provocative words: 'N.B. The author assures you, he thinks this is the best English Dictionary in the World.'

Certain biographers and critics have quoted that apparently fatuous boast without giving Wesley's own comment and without pointing out that, until Johnson's abridged dictionary appeared some years later, Wesley's was actually the best small dictionary of English. But his comment is as delightful as it is shrewd; indeed the whole preface should find a place in any comprehensive anthology of English prose. Referring to that title-page challenge, Wesley remarks: 'I have so often observed, the only way, according to the modern taste, for any author to procure commendation to his book is, vehemently to commend it himself. For want of this deference to the publick, several excellent tracts lately printed, but left to commend themselves by their intrinsic worth, are utterly unknown or forgotten. Whereas if a writer of tolerable sense will but bestow a few violent encomiums on his own work, especially if they are skilfully ranged in the title-page, it will pass thro' six editions in a trice; the world being too complaisant to give a gentleman the Lie, and taking it for granted, he understands his own performance best. In compliance therefore with the taste of the age, I add, that this little dictionary is not only the shortest and the cheapest, but likewise, by many degrees, the most correct which is extant at this day. Many are the mistakes in all the other *English* dictionaries which I have yet seen. Whereas I can truly say, I know of none in this; and I conceive the reader will believe me: for if I had, I should not have left it there. Use then this help, till you find a better.' Much the same tone of raillery informs the note to the 2nd edition: ' In this Edition I have added some hundreds of words, which were omitted in the former: chiefly from Mr. *Johnson's* dictionary, which I carefully looked over for that purpose. And I will now venture to affirm, that, small as it is, this dictionary is quite sufficient, for enabling any one to understand the best Writings now extant, in the *English* tongue.'

Wesley in many ways followed the older English lexicographers, who—and this holds till the eighteenth century—aimed not at completeness but at explaining the more difficult words. In 1616 Dr. John Bullokar published his ' English Expositour ', the next year saw Minsheu's remarkable ' Guide into the Tongues ' (the first English etymological dictionary), Cockeram's much more modest ' Interpreter ' appeared in 1723,

Blount's 'Glossographia' in 1656; in 1678 came what is often considered the first English dictionary in the modern sense, that compiled by Edward Phillips, the nephew of Milton—'New World of Words', often re-edited by the industrious and by no means foolish John Kersey; but it was Nathaniel Bailey who in 1730 (the smaller edition of 1721 followed the selective principle) brought out a *complete* dictionary, i.e. one admitting *dog*, *cat*, *the*, *of*, and so forth. It was Bailey who held the field for thirty-five years—until, in fact, Johnson, drawing largely on his work, put an end to his supremacy.[1] Wesley's first edition came out just in time to avoid being annihilated by the Doctor's magistral dictionary, whose appearance nevertheless prevented Wesley's little book from winning the popularity it deserved; *Johnson* was to the eighteenth century what *Webster* became for the next and *Wyld* may become for our own.

Wesley's aim and method cannot be described better than in his own words. 'As incredible as it may appear,' he begins his preface, 'I must avow, that this dictionary is not published to get money, but to assist persons of common sense and no learning to understand the best *English* authors; and that, with as little expense of time or money, as the nature of the thing would allow.' He continues thus: 'To this end it contains, not a heap of *Greek* and *Latin* words, just tagged with *English* terminations (for no good *English* writer, none but vain or senseless pedants,

---

[1] I owe these facts (the list, I may add, is not complete) to the fascinating essay 'On Dictionaries' in Professor Ernest Weekley's suggestive and entertaining volume, 'Adjectives and Other Words' (1st edition, 1930).

give these any place in their writings :) not a scroll of barbarous *law expressions*, which are neither *Greek, Latin*, nor good *English* : not a crowd of *technical* terms, the meaning whereof is to be sought in books expressly wrote on the subjects to which they belong : not such *English* words as *and, of, but* [1] . . . ; but " most of those hard words which are found in the best *English* writers ".' He adds that he likewise omits ' all, the meaning of which may be easily gathered from those of the same derivation ' ; the whole with a view to convenience of size and to cheapness.

Wesley's dictionary was, within its self-imposed limits, a very able piece of work. On account of its omission of the small coin of speech, it was useless to foreigners—unless they happened to possess the rudiments. Nor was it meant for scholars, as the absence of etymologies, illustrative phrases, and illustrative passages (these last were to be introduced by Johnson), and all references to lexicographers will show. But for the ordinary ' man of sense ', whom he rightly assumed to be indifferent to erudition and encyclopaedizing, Wesley succeeded in producing a very serviceable dictionary.

His spelling is occasionally irregular, as in *burser, dipthong*, and the differentiation of *accessary* and *accessory*. There are also, of course, spellings that were current in the eighteenth century but now obsolete, such as *asphaltus* and *atchieve*. The eighteenth-century note appears further in some of the definitions. *Abscess* is ' an imposthume ' ; *behemoth*, ' the river-horse '

[1] Nor the *cat* and *dog, door* and *bed, ah* and *oh, run* and *see* varieties.

(hippopotamus); *buxom* is 'pliant, wanton, merry', and it reminds us that it is extremely unwise in the United States to describe a woman as 'buxom'; *campaign* is 'a summer's war', for fighting was not carried on in the winter months; *decimate* is 'to take tithe'; *epicure* means 'a glutton, a sensual man'; 'one skilled in Hebrew' is not a *Hebraist* as now, but a *Hebrician*; *meretricious* is bluntly 'whorish', without any modern frills; *philology* is 'the study of polite literature: criticism'; *romantic* is 'such as is described in romances: wild'; *vapid* is 'dead (spoken of drink)'.

Wesley, though rarely vague, is often reticent, sex being for the most part eschewed, though there are several words for a homosexual. He is brief and to the point: a dictionary is 'a book explaining the words of a language', a glossary 'a dictionary to show the sense of words in several languages'; and usually he is much briefer than that. Although he aims not at wit, nor at originality, some of his definitions, either intrinsically or with reference to his life and work, call for quotation. An *enthusiast* is 'a religious madman, one that fancies himself inspired' (Wesley knew that he was often described thus), while a *visionary* is 'one that sees, or pretends to, visions' (he was aware that he numbered a few among his followers); if a *Latitudinarian* means 'one that fancies all religions are saving', a *Methodist* denotes 'one that lives according to the method laid down in the Bible'. *Anecdotes* are 'secret histories' (biography *à la Maurois*); *memoirs* 'a plain history' (annals, in short); *grammar* is 'the art of speaking and writing properly', *figure* 'an elegantly-uncommon way of speaking', and *rhapsody* signifies ' a confused collection of words '. *Alchymy* is narrowed down to ' the art of changing one metal into another ' ; *astrology* is ' the (supposed) art of foretelling things by the stars '. *Bastille* is ' the state-prison in Paris ' ; *Olympus* ' a poetical name for heaven '. A *coquet* is ' a woman affectedly airy, seeking to make conquests '. A *tarantula* is ' a venomous spider, whose bite can be cured only by music ' (especially that of the *tarantella*), which links up with *tarantism*, the modern name for dancing mania—not confined to *Taranto*. *Ventilator* is ' an engine to bring fresh air into any place ', and *refrigerate* means nothing more chilly than ' to cool '.

The scope of Wesley's dictionary can best be gauged, however, by a comparison with some modern work ; for this purpose the ' Pocket Oxford '[1] will serve admirably. The number of words treated by Wesley is about 5,200, that by the ' Pocket Oxford ' about 19,000,[2] but if we bear in mind the express omissions in the earlier work, we notice that the two dictionaries are (dates remembered) practically equivalent. At *Q* we find only thirty words in Wesley, just four times that number in the ' Pocket Oxford ' ; *X* in Wesley supplies only two entries (*xenodochium* and *xystus*), in the modern work six (*x, Xanthippe, xebec, xi, xylonite, xylophone*) ; *Y* in Wesley yields three words, in the other sixty ; *Z* seven and thirty-eight respectively. (The learned and technical element is noticeable in the last two letters of the modern dictionary.)

[1] I use the 1st edition (1924). Edited by F. G. and H. W. Fowler.
[2] By headings ; cognates and derivatives listed under a main word are ignored in this estimate.

The manner of definition can likewise be seen best from a few brief samples, in which, again, we must be careful to remember the difference in aim between these two dictionaries. *Debilitate*, says Wesley, is ' to weaken ', the Fowler brothers (the War most unfortunately removed one of them) are equally terse with ' to cause debility in ', but then they have previously defined *debility*. In Wesley, *fabric* means only ' a building ', in the Fowlers a ' thing put together ; building ; structure ; (also *textile fabric*) woven material '. The former defines *professor* as ' a public reader of lectures ', the latter as a ' person making profession (of a religion, &c.), holder of university chair or other teacher of high rank '. *Student* in the earlier is ' a scholar, studious man ', in the later— well, the entry is rather too long to be given here.

Wesley has this in common with the Fowlers, as with such other notable dictionary-makers as Minsheu, Johnson, Weekley : he imprints on a book that the unthinking expect to be dryasdust and tedious a character at once unmistakable, personal, and enjoyable : for only the superhumanly conscientious or perhaps rather the portentously solemn among lexicographers can resist being personal now and again. It is certainly to our advantage that personality, humour and wit do thus break the bounds of erudition in Wesley and those others.

JOHNSON'S DICTIONARY

DR. SAMUEL JOHNSON, 1709-84, compiled the most famous dictionary of any country or time. The seven greatest dictionaries of the English tongue are Skinner's 'Etymologicon', 1671; Nathan Bailey's 'Dictionary', 1721; Johnson's, 1755; Webster's various dictionaries, considered as one, 1806 to 1834; 'The Century Dictionary', edited by William D. Whitney, 1889-91; and 'The Oxford Dictionary', edited by Sir James Murray, Dr. Henry Bradley, Sir William Craigie, and Dr. C. T. Onions, 1884-1928; and lastly the two-volumed 'Shorter Oxford Dictionary', edited by Dr. Onions, assisted by the late William Little, Mr. H. W. Fowler and Mrs. J. Coulson. It may be remarked that Webster and Whitney were Americans. Also that there was much overlapping of popularity: Skinner was often used by Johnson for his etymologies; Bailey's dictionary reached its 24th edition in 1782, or twenty-seven years after the appearance of Johnson's; Johnson's itself, as re-edited by Archdeacon Todd about 1817, held the field against Webster till about 1840; 'Webster' modernized still has no rival as a one-volume dictionary;[1] the 'Century Dictionary' even now is often

[1] Professor H. C. Wyld's 'Universal Dictionary' stands midway between 'Webster' and those two admirable 'desk' dictionaries, the 'Concise Oxford' and Chambers's 'Twentieth Century'. Webster has a close rival (*proxime accessit*) in *Funk and Wagnalls*, also American.

preferred by scholars who cannot afford to buy and who cannot easily consult the gigantic 'Oxford Dictionary'; the 'Oxford' is the finest dictionary ever published—or likely to be published—and even now Sir William Craigie, and more especially Dr. Onions (for Sir William is in the U.S.A. directing the formation of a dictionary of American-English), are preparing a Supplement that will bring the twenty imposing volumes up to date.

Of all these, Johnson was the most remarkable as a man. Since it was Professor (later Sir) Walter Raleigh who did much to restore him to his rightful position, let us quote from those admirable 'Six Essays on Johnson' which remind us that Raleigh himself, though he did not write very much, was likewise, in a more limited circle, greatly admired and respected and loved. 'The world'—and Raleigh was no mere cloistered nor secluded scholar—'is not so constructed that a fool, by sheer force of loquacity and indiscretion, can make a pompous old dogmatist into one of the great live figures of history. A man of profound humanity and conquering intellect lived a private life in London, never seeking public fame or exalted company, content to amuse his leisured hours with the conversation of his friends. So great was the force of his mind and character that he became famous in spite of himself, and his lightest sayings were treasured and chronicled by those about him. . . . It was not Boswell who made Johnson; it was Johnson who, by his wealth of tenderness and sympathy, his understanding of the human situation, its joys and sorrows, awoke in the breast of his own generation a response which, diffused at first and speaking in many voices, at last gathered strength and definiteness, and expressed itself in the voice of James Boswell.'

It was, if I remember aright, Macaulay who said that, while most authors are kept in the public memory by their books, Johnson's books are remembered because of Johnson. This is not to state that Johnson was not a very remarkable man of letters: his dictionary, two or three shortish poems, the four or five best of his essays, his novel ' Rasselas ', ' The Lives of the Poets ', and the Introduction to his edition of Shakespeare, give the lie very forcibly to any such contention, and either his dictionary or the ' Lives ' would put him at the very head of the list were he writing to-day.

Part of Johnson's hold on the admiration of Englishmen results from the fact that he possessed many of those essentially British virtues and qualities which we English value and by which we English are— what we are. ' The unusual combination of these qualities with those of a scholar, and a wit, and a writer-of-all-work, eminent for the force and dignity of his pen, contribute to give Johnson his unique position ' in his own age ; and, to amplify the words of that poor lecturer but admirable scholar and most likable man, the late Thomas Seccombe, that position rightly has much to do with the esteem in which Johnson is now held.

Another admirable scholar and most cultured man of letters, the late Sir Edmund Gosse (who once told me that he was very sorry to notice that I had not read some one of his books—I now forget which, but I do know that I immediately repaired so tactless an omission), has written so pertinently on this subject of the charm exercised by Johnson over the nineteenth century—it is true that Sir Edmund actually penned the passage in 1888—that I must quote him :

'He talked superb literature freely for thirty years, and all England listened ; he grew to be the centre of literary opinion, and he was so majestic in intellect, so honest in purpose, so kind and pure in heart, so full of humour and reasonable sweetness, and yet so trenchant, and at need so grim, that he never sank to be the figure-head of a clique, nor ever lost the balance of sympathy with readers of every rank and age. His influence was so wide, and withal so wholesome, that literary life in this country has never been since his day what it was before it. He has made the more sordid parts of its weakness shameful, and he has raised a standard of personal conduct that everyone admits. He was a gruff old bear, "Ursa Major", but it would surely be hard to find the man or woman, whose opinion is worth having, who does not love almost more than revere the memory of Sam Johnson.'

Much of his reputation as a writer and as a man is based on, or connected with, 'A Dictionary of the English Language, in which the words are deduced from their originals and illustrated in their different significations by examples from the best writers'. The work had in 1747 been dedicated to Lord Chesterfield ; it appeared on 15 April 1755 in two volumes (folio), price four guineas. Chesterfield may have rather neglected Johnson, who wrote a most arresting letter to his 'patron' : that letter is famous, too famous. It is but fair to Chesterfield to say that his 'offence' was not one: this has been clearly shown by the late and much lamented Charles Whibley in an essay published in 'The Criterion', 1924, and again by Mr. Bonamy Dobrée in his magnificent edition of Chesterfield's Letters.

The illustrative passages were an innovation, and Johnson succeeded, to an astonishing extent, in fixing the correct senses contemporary with his labours. He was the first 'English' lexicographer who was not a mere drudge nor yet only a scholar; he was a real man and an all-round man of letters. He did not record everything: in other words, he reserved the right to select his vocabulary. His influence may be said to have given English a set vocabulary for fifty years, but he did not flatter himself either that he would do this or that it was desirable that he should. In the profound and human Preface, he wisely wrote: ' Sounds are too volatile and subtile for legal restraints; to enchain syllables, and to lash the wind, are equally the undertakings of pride, unwilling to measure its desires by its strength.' He was, however, mistaken enough to attempt to banish colloquial idioms and to brand them as either ' low ' or ' ungrammatical '; he wished indeed ' to refine our language to grammatical purity, and to clear it from colloquial barbarisms, licentious idioms, and irregular combinations'. As Mr. Logan Pearsall Smith in his admirable and most readable book, ' Words and Idioms ', has observed: ' Although this point of view is now an obsolete one, . . . we are still a little influenced by the eighteenth-century attitude towards idiom, although we have ceased to believe in the reasons for that attitude.' The same writer points out that

Johnson hated such verbs as 'bind up', 'bring in', 'look on', and that he went so far as to declare 'to come by' (to obtain) to be 'an irregular and improper use'; finding this phrasal verb in Hooker, Shakespeare, Bacon and Dryden, he admitted that it had 'very powerful authorities'.

'For pronunciation', says Johnson, 'the best general rule is, to consider those the most elegant speakers who deviate least from the written words.' Johnson, in brief, favoured a 'regular and solemn' rather than a 'cursory and colloquial' pronunciation. (For an illuminating paragraph, see Professor Henry Cecil Wyld's 'History of Modern Colloquial English'.)

But we have omitted to mention the experiences that Johnson had in the preparation of his dictionary: and who can describe them better than the lexicographer himself? 'When first I engaged in this work', he relates in the Preface, 'I resolved to leave neither words nor things unexamined, and pleased myself with a prospect of the hours which I should revel away in feasts of literature. . . . When I had thus enquired into the original of words, I resolved to show likewise my attention to things; to pierce deep into every science, to enquire the nature of every substance . . . to limit every idea by a definition strictly logical, and exhibit every production of art or nature in an accurate description, that my book might be in the place of all other dictionaries whether appellative or technical. But these were the dreams of a poet doomed at last to wake a lexicographer. . . . To deliberate whenever I doubted, to enquire whenever I was ignorant, would have protracted the undertaking without end, and, perhaps, without much improvement. . . . I saw that one enquiry only gave occasion to another, that book referred to book, that to search was not always to find, and to find was not always to be informed. . . . I then contracted my design, determining to confide in myself, and no longer to solicit auxiliaries, which produced more incumbrance than assistance : by this I obtained at least one advantage, that I set limits to my work, which would in time be ended, though not completed.' With six assistants, Johnson spent about eight years on his dictionary. And he lived to revise four editions of it.

His origins and derivations were often wrong. ' It may be doubted ', writes Professor Ernest Weekley (whose ' Etymological Dictionary of Modern English ' is as full of originality and character as Johnson's itself), ' whether there was ever a worse etymologist than Dr. Johnson. He was a good classic, but completely ignorant of the earlier history of the Teutonic languages.' He even made an occasional mistake in definition : ' pastern ' defined as 'the knee of a horse ' ; both ' leeward ' and ' windward ' described as ' towards the wind ' ; ' cricket ' as ' a sport, at which the contenders drive a ball with sticks in opposition to each other '—evidently a sort of hockey. He sometimes slipped into ' Johnsonese ', as when he defined a cough as ' a convulsion of the lungs, vellicated by some sharp serosity '. Occasionally he made a mistake that, on the strength of his authority, has become accepted, such as ' conservancy ' for the correct ' conservacy '. But, as Professor Weekley —from whose delightful ' Adjectives and Other Words ' I take these convenient examples—would be the first to admit, Johnson was a very great lexicographer.

To turn over the pages of Johnson's dictionary (copies of the later editions are quite cheap) is to pay so many visits to the more than worthy doctor, and scores of definitions attest that 'This was a man!' Kindliness, humour, a profound sense of justice, hatred of hypocrisy and sham, courage,—these and other qualities abound. When some young ladies thanked him for omitting indecent words, he replied with a laugh, 'So, my dears, you have been looking for them.' It is related, on credible authority, that the Commissioners of Excise were so annoyed by his definition of 'excise' that they consulted the Attorney-General to see if an action could not be brought against the dictionary; and that definition might, with one modification, serve as a slogan for those who object to paying income-tax : 'EXCISE : a hateful tax levied upon commodities, and adjudged not by the common judges of property, but wretches hired by those to whom excise is paid.'

Johnson was a Tory. He was also a very scornful contemner of the political morals of the day. That scorn appears in the definition of a pension as 'an allowance paid to anyone without an equivalent ; in England it is generally understood to mean pay given to a state hireling for treason to his country '. He thought, but did not say so in his dictionary, that the first Whig was the Devil and that patriotism (a patriot in the true sense he himself was, of course) constitutes 'the last refuge of a scoundrel', an epigram that the disaffected would err greatly in considering to be tantamount to the implicit teaching of (say) the talking-film version of 'All Quiet on the Western Front': 'the most disgraceful of all deaths is to die for one's country'. So much depends on the country. Which reminds me of Johnson's definition of 'oats': 'A grain, which in England is generally given to horses, but in Scotland supports the people.' Promptly a Scotsman replied: 'And where will you find such horses or such men?'

A FALSTAFF AMONG ANTIQUARIES

I

ONE of the most entertaining figures of the eighteenth century was Captain Francis Grose,[1] who appears to have been born early in 1731 and who is known to have died in 1791. Although, like the greatest of English historians, he saw no active service, he yet had a very sound knowledge of the Army and all that therein is. 'Stout and burly Captain Grose' was the greatest antiquary, the most inveterate and successful joker, and the best porter-drinker of his century: he must have been a remarkable man on any one of these three counts. He was famous and—rare combination—harmlessly notorious.

His father, a Swiss, settled in England early in the eighteenth century and went to live at Richmond in Surrey; he prospered as a jeweller. Francis, after a classical education, did not, as one might have expected, go to a university (only Oxford and Cambridge existed in England at that time), but studied art. In 1766 he was elected a member of the Incorporated Society of Artists. From June 1755

[1] A fuller account of the man and his work is appended to my edition of Grose's 'Vulgar Tongue' (Oxford University Press, 1931).

until 1763 he was the Richmond Herald. Thence he passed to the adjutancy and paymastership of the Hampshire Militia, where, according to his own story, his only account-books were his right-hand and left-hand pockets : into the one he put all moneys received, from the other he drew all necessary expenses : that he was anything but a rogue is clear from the fact that it was at this period that he ran through a considerable patrimony. Nor was his sense of honour or his reputation for sterling honesty ever doubted. After a long period of research work (conducted on liberal and jovial lines) interspersed with travel in search of knowledge and curiosities, he held a captaincy and adjutancy in the Surrey Militia from 1778 till his death. From 1773 to 1787 he published his greatest work, 'The Antiquities of England and Wales'; in 1785 his 'Classical Dictionary of the Vulgar Tongue'; in the following year his valuable 'Military Antiquities' (especially of the English Army); in 1787, 'A Provincial Glossary', the materials of which he had been collecting for many years in the course of his other investigations. In 1789 he toured Scotland, where he was quizzed and fêted by his fellow-antiquaries and where he met and delighted Robert Burns ('of whom more anon', to avail oneself of a fatally convenient cliché); that he worked hard, as well as playing boyishly, is proved by 'The Antiquities of Scotland' (1789-90). Early in 1791 he issued a volume of essays entitled 'The Grumbler', and in the spring he set out on that tour of Ireland which ended in the grave, apoplexy taking him off while he dined at Dublin with his friend Nathaniel Hone. A friend completed and, not long after Grose's death, published 'The Antiquities of Ireland'.

Francis Grose was the gayest of a capable family. Of his four brothers, one wrote a very tolerable book on Ethics; another, a 'Voyage to the East Indies' (1757), which met with esteem as well as success; the third was knighted for his services to the Law, while the fourth did well for himself in Threadneedle Street. His two sons were soldiers, the one dying in India, the other becoming Deputy-Governor of New South Wales, whence some kind soul may one day send me a large amount of hitherto unpublished material concerning the governor's vastly more interesting father.

The most reliable character-sketch of Grose is that by his friend and occasional 'silent' collaborator, the Rev. Mark Noble: 'His figure was more of Sancho Panza than Falstaff; he partook greatly of the qualities of both. He was as low, squat and rotund as the former, and not less a sloven; equalled him, too, in his love of sleep, and nearly so in his proverbs. In his wit he was a Falstaff. He was the butt for other men to shoot at, but it always rebounded with a double force. He could eat with Sancho, and drink with the Knight. In simplicity, probity and a compassionate heart, he was wholly the Panza breed; his jocularity could have pleased a prince. His learning, sense, science and honour might have secured him the favour, not the rejection, of the all-accomplished conqueror of France, Henry V. 'An inimitable boon-companion,' adds Noble.

So boon that he won the heart of Burns, who, for

him, wrote his masterpiece, *Tam o' Shanter*, and about him wrote that amusing poem which, quotable only in parts, begins :

> Hear, Land o' Cakes and brither Scots,
> Frae Maidenkirk to Johnny Groat's ;
> If there's a hole in a' your coats,
>   I rede you tent it ;
> A chiel's amang you, taking notes,
>   And, faith, he'll prent it.

The last statement has become almost proverbial among the allusive and the literary for any very observant author. Burns goes on to call Grose a man ' o' stature short, but genius bright ', and he ends by declaring him to be ' a dainty chiel '.

An excellent portrait of the corpulent, bright-eyed, double-chinned, enormous-calved, exceedingly broad-shouldered, roguish-pleasing antiquary was made by Dance. Another (artist unknown) had under it lines, written by one of the Antiquarian Society, that referred to his weakness for sleep :

> Now [Grose], like bright Phoebus, is sunk into rest,
> Society droops for the loss of his jest ;
> Antiquarian debates, unoccasion'd with mirth,
> To genius and learning will never give birth.
> Then wake, brother member, our friend from his sleep,
> Lest Apollo should frown, and Bacchus should weep.

Grose was also a notable artist ; he exhibited at the Royal Academy, illustrated his own books, and devised—with illustrations more than clever—some remarkably pithy and competent rules for drawing caricatures. His most solid fame rests on his anti-quarianism ; his sprightliest title to consideration is his dictionary of slang, as consistently valuable as it is occasionally audacious.

II

Perhaps more interesting than Captain Grose the man was Francis Grose, F.S.A., the scholar and antiquary. And his most interesting work was the ' Classical Dictionary of the Vulgar Tongue ', which, published in 1785, contained slang, colloquialisms, and thieves' language. It is a ripe, witty, and in parts a Rabelaisian book ; it has a rare good-humour ; it carries its formidable learning with the light agility that characterized the personal carriage of this corpulent man.

This dictionary is the better of the only two adequate lexicons of English cant [1]—the language of thieves and other criminals, of gypsies and other vagrants. It is also the earliest noteworthy dictionary of the more colloquial English speech. But the proof of the pudding is in the examples.

ACORN : You will ride a horse foaled by an acorn ; i.e. the gallows, called also the Wooden and Three-legged Mare. You will be hanged. (Grose has, at *Newgate*, an entry that makes one shudder.)

BAD BARGAIN : One of his majesty's bad bargains ; a worthless soldier, a malingeror. (The sort of which one hears so much in the War novels.)

---

[1] The writer has in preparation a dictionary of Cant in the English tongue : for this historical and comparative work, which is very difficult to compile, he will be grateful for any assistance that the charitable may feel moved to give him.

A FALSTAFF AMONG ANTIQUARIES

BAKER'S DOZEN : Fourteen ; that number of rolls being allowed to the purchasers of a dozen. (No longer, alas !)

BEDFORDSHIRE : I am for Bedfordshire, i.e. for going to bed. (The wit of half-wits.)

BESS, or BETTY : A small instrument used by housebreakers to force open doors. Bring bess and glim ; bring the instrument to force the door, and the dark lantern. Small flasks like those for Florence wine are also called Betties. ('Open doors' don't need forcing : the first duty of a lexicographer is to avoid ambiguity ; the second golden rule is to be simple, e.g. to say 'a dictionary-maker's first duty is to be clear'.—The sex of the instrument has changed ; it is now called a jemmy.)

CANTING : Preaching with a whining, affected tone, perhaps a corruption of chaunting ; some derive it from Andrew Cant, a famous Scotch preacher, who used that whining manner of expression. Also a kind of gibberish used by thieves and gypsies, called likewise pedlar's French, the slang, &c. &c. (There were, in point of fact, two famous preachers named Cant ; but the word is connected with *chant.*)

CATCH PENNY : Any temporary contrivance to raise a contribution on the public.

CHALKERS : Men of wit in Ireland, who in the night amuse themselves with cutting inoffensive passengers across the face with a knife. They are somewhat like those facetious gentlemen some time ago known in England by the title of Sweaters and Mohocks. (These last jolly little fellows flourished about the year 1710. Swift, trenchant as usual, remarks : '. . . a race called the mohocks that play the devil about this town every night.')

CHERUBIMS : Peevish children, because cherubims and seraphims continually do cry. (The last three words are a Biblical quotation. Grose uses the 'double plural'; the learned plurals of *cherub* and *seraph* are *cherubim* and *seraphim*.)

EMPEROR : Drunk as an emperor, i.e. ten times as drunk as a lord. ('Blind', in fact.)

FLASH LINGO : The canting or slang language.

FRENCH CREAM : Brandy ; so called by the old tabbies and dowagers when [it is] drunk in their tea.

FURMEN : Aldermen. (A reference to their ceremonial dress.)

GENTLEMAN COMMONER : An empty bottle ; a university joke, gentlemen commoners not being deemed over-full of learning. (Just as *a dead marine* is a sailor's joke at the expense of the amphibious marine.)

GENTLEMAN OF THREE OUTS : That is, without money, without wit, and without manners ; some add another out, i.e. without credit. (A pun for the initiate.)

GLUE POT : A parson ; from joining men and women together in matrimony. (As if it were his fault. . . .)

GRUB STREET : A street near Moorfields, formerly the supposed habitation of many persons who wrote for the booksellers : hence a Grub-street writer means a hackney author, who manufactures books for the booksellers. (Now he does it, only too often, for the publishers.)

A FALSTAFF AMONG ANTIQUARIES

GRUB STREET NEWS : Lying intelligence. (How times have changed !)

HABERDASHER OF PRONOUNS : A schoolmaster, or usher. (Another eighteenth-century name was *Syntax*, whence William Combe's allegedly humorous poem, ' The Three Tours of Dr. Syntax '.)

HARE : He has swallowed a hare ; he is drunk ; more probably a *hair*, which requires washing down. (A tip from one who knew.)

HICK : A country hick ; an ignorant clown. (Usually supposed to be American, as any ' moviefan ' will tell you.)

IRISH BEAUTY : A woman with two black eyes. (Written, of course, before Grose went to Ireland in 1791.)

LAND PIRATES : Highwaymen. (Due to Shakespearean influence.)

LINGO : Language. An outlandish lingo ; a foreign tongue. The parlezvous lingo ; the French language. (Probably from *lingua franca*, the mongrel Esperanto of the Mediterranean.)

MELLOW : Almost drunk.

QUEER BIRDS : Rogues relieved from prison, and returned to their old trade. (Nowadays, a *queer bird* is an *odd fish*.)

QUOD : Newgate, or any other prison. The dab's in quod ; [thieves' language for] the poor rogue is in prison.

RED LATTICE : A public-house.

RESURRECTION MEN : Persons employed by the students in anatomy to steal dead bodies out of churchyards.

RHINO : Money. (The popularity of the thing has ensured the permanence of the name.)

ROARATORIOS and UPROARS : Oratorios and operas.

ROW : A disturbance : a term used by the students at Cambridge.

RUMPUS : A riot, a quarrel, or confusion.

SAINT : A piece of spoilt timber in a coach-maker's shop ; like a saint, devoted to the flames.

SCANDAL BROTH : Tea. (To-day the vulgar male would call it a *hen-party*.)

SCOUT : A college errand-boy at Oxford, called a gyp at Cambridge. Also a watchman or a watch.

SMOKER : A tobacconist.

SPIFLICATE : To confound, silence, or dumbfound. (Often used to intimidate children, who think that nothing short of murder can possibly be meant.)

SPOIL-PUDDING : A parson who preaches long sermons, keeping his congregation in church till the puddings are overdone. (Compare *spoil-sport* and the old-fashioned *trouble-feast*.)

STINGO : Strong beer, or other liquor.

TILBURY : Sixpence : so called from its formerly being the fare for crossing over from Gravesend to Tilbury fort.

TOPPING FELLOW : One at the top or head of his profession.

TRIB. A prison : perhaps from tribulation. (For *perhaps*, read *certainly*.)

TUFT HUNTER : A university parasite, one who courts the acquaintance of nobility, whose caps are adorned with a gold tuft.

VAMPERS : Stockings. (Still the stock-in-trade of vamps : pun most execrable !)

WHITE TAPE : Geneva. (I.e. gin.)

WORD-PECKER : A punster, one who plays on words. (Compare *word-grubber*, a critic who can't see the wood for the trees.)

YELLOW BOYS : Guineas. (Later, any gold coin.)

III
ASPECTS OF SOLDIERS' SLANG: 1914-18

BRITISH SOLDIERS' SLANG WITH A PAST

I. THE CLERGY, THE LAW, DRINKING, THEFT

THIS essay [1] concerns only such Army slang words, and far from all such words, as have a history and an origin at least as far back as 1880.

It is instructive to turn to Weekley's 'Etymological Dictionary of Modern English'. In the Preface, which bears the date of September 1920, we hear that there has been an influx of foreign words and that 'among such foreign words are many neologisms due to the Great War, a certain number of which may successfully resist that demobilization of the war-words which is now actively proceeding. The more recondite foreign technicalities of war have been avoided, but the Anglo-Indian vocabulary of the British Army, much of which is already to be found in the works of Mr. Kipling and other Anglo-Indian writers, has been drawn upon freely'. Many Army slang words and phrases of 1914–18 are now forgotten, though it would seem that a very fair number will survive.

As to the slang that arose in India, nearly all of it dates from the period of the Indian Mutiny or from the subsequent and constant occupation of India by the British Army. Perhaps the only words that are

[1] For other groups of words, see Appendix II.

more than a century old are *wallah* and some of its compounds. Meaning man, fellow, the word appears in print as early as 1776 as *Agra wallah*, a native of Agra; as *patriot-wallah* in 1785. In 1914–18 *wallah* usually designated an officer with a specific job, as, for example, a *Lewis Gun wallah*. One occasionally heard the phrase *an amen-wallah*, a clergyman, especially a chaplain, but originally a chaplain's clerk; this compound may have been formed by some scholarly soldier that knew the eighteenth-century *amen-curler*, a parish clerk. The usual Army word for a parson was, of course, *padre*, which, from Latin *pater*, is in three Romance languages the title applied to the regular clergy, and in India, via the Portuguese, to a minister or priest of any Christian religion; hence, a chaplain in either the Army or the Navy. Apparently the word first appeared in English literature in 1584, but it was two centuries, or more, before it became at all frequent in the relevant sense.

Bad bargain has long been in general slang use for a bad soldier, and its general application to any disadvantageous arrangement dates back to the sixteenth century. Not at any time much used by soldiers, it was originally the *King's bad bargain*; in 1785, Grose, the soldier antiquary and lexicographer, defines thus: 'a malingeror, a soldier who shirks his duty'. The same authority has the common army and civilian word *beak*, 'a justice of peace, or magistrate'; the word occurs in Harman's 'Caveat for Common Cursetors' in 1573 as *beck*; yet probably it is connected with *beak*, a bird's bill, and, like so much early cant (the slang of thieves and other criminals, gypsies and other vagrants and vagabonds), was perhaps due to those university men who ran wild in London : I suggest that *beck*, as an anglicized form of the French *bec*, is basically the same as, and afterwards became, *beak*. *Binge*, in pre-War days an Oxford University word for a drinking bout, was developed by the soldiers to mean ' an expedition deliberately undertaken in company for the purpose of relieving depression, celebrating an occasion, or a spasm of high spirits, by becoming intoxicated. But music and singing are essentially part of a binge. More an officers' word than a private soldier's ' (John Brophy : ' Songs and Slang of the British Soldier : 1914-1918 '). In 1914-18 the word was usually a noun, rarely a verb ; it appears in neither the ' Oxford English Dictionary ' nor Weekley's ' Etymological Dictionary '.[1] The word may be due to a confusion and combining of the Lincolnshire *binge*, to soak,[2] and the cant *bingo*, defined as ' brandy or other spirituous liquor ' by Grose, who has also *bingo mort*, cant for a female dram-drinker, and *bingo boy*, cant for a male dram-drinker ; as Brophy (l.c.) points out, the latter term is interesting ' in view of *The Bing Boys*, a very popular musical comedy in 1916-17 which made famous the song, " Another little drink wouldn't do us any harm ".' Dr. Murray in 1888 suggested that *bingo* was *b* (for brandy) + *stingo* ; very diffidently I suggest that a Lincolnshire wit gave to *binge*, to soak, the termination *o* (after deleting *e*) on the analogy of the much older slang *stingo* (from *sting*), strong ale or beer, apparently

[1] After this : the O.E.D. ; Weekley.
[2] Cf. the sea-slang phrase, *to binge a cask*, ' to get the remaining liquor from the wood by rinsing it with water '—' Sea Slang ', by Frank C. Bowen, 1930.

first used in print, and perhaps coined by, Randolph about 1635. Another civilian slang word, *bitch*, to spoil, ruin, was vigorously adopted by the soldier; this sense is modern, but it probably derives from the eighteenth-century use, to hang back.

As one would expect, the idea of theft and illicit acquisition forms a significant group of soldiers' slang words: *bone, make, nab, nail, pinch, scrounge, snaffle, win*, to mention only those which originated before 1830. *Bone* is inadequately treated in the O.E.D., for in the 5th edition of Dyche's illuminating 'Dictionary', 1748, we read that it is 'a cant word, to seize or arrest; also to cheat or strip a person of his money or goods', while Grose, 1788, defines *boned* as 'seized, apprehended, taken up by a constable. Cant'; in 1914–18 the verb meant either to steal (or merely borrow with no very firm intention of restoring) or to arrest. The origin is dubious: it may be a figure of speech based on a dog's removal of a bone to a place of safety, or a corruption of *bonnet* (a gambling shark), or again a sense-development of that literal meaning, to deprive of the bone, to take the bones from, which has been current since the fifteenth century: the second theory is improbable, for it implies a pun (*to bonnet*, to bone it) that requires the already-existent use of *bone* = to take an important part of, thence to take the whole: whereby we cursorily indicate the probable origin, for the dog-metaphor explanation seems very thin. *Make*, likewise thieves' cant, appears in B.E.'s 'Dictionary of the Canting Crew', 1690 and again in Grose, in the modern sense, to steal; the word implied cunning or skill in the acquiring. *Nab*, established early in the seventeenth century, is cant and dialectal for to seize a person or to steal a thing, though in its early days it had, in many phrases, the more general senses to take, receive, get ; in cant, *to nab the stoop* signified to stand in the pillory. *Nail* was used both for to take without hesitation and to steal. Chaucer had it to signify simply to take ; in the eighteenth century the verb denoted securing, ' fixing ' an offer ; Vaux in 1819 records it, ' to nail is to rob or steal ' ; in this last sense, the word is either low slang or thieves' cant. *Pinch* in 1914-18 likewise meant to arrest or to steal ; both senses were current in thieves' slang in the seventeenth century. *Scrounge* is one of the most famous War words : both the name and the thing were excessively common, and one said *on the scrounge*, on the look-out for anything materially advantageous, and *to scrounge*, ' to steal, not personal belongings, but from a department or some other embodiment of authority. More army property changed hands by scrounging than by legitimate means. Also used intransitively *to scrounge about*, to go seeking an opportunity of stealing, either a particular article or whatever fortune offered ' (Brophy, op. cit.). The word is not in Hotten, nor in Farmer and Henley ; Weekley and the O.E.D. are, unintentionally, a little vague ; the real solvent is supplied by the late and much lamented Joseph Wright, who, in his ' English Dialect Dictionary ', makes it clear [1] that it is a North Country word, that one of the secondary meanings is ' to wander about idly ', and that one of the meanings of the noun is ' a thorough search '. A

[1] If we take his examples along with the provincial *scrunge*, to steal (generally unripe) apples and pears (J. Redding Ware : ' Passing English ', 1912.)

scrounger, which I believe to be a War-time neologism, is of course an adept at this valuable art. *Snaffle*, to steal, was defined by Hotten as to arrest, but this sense is obsolete. ' The New Canting Dictionary ', 1725, says, ' To steal, to rob, to purloin ', but that the word was in use considerably earlier may be inferred from the fact that already in 1700 a *snaffler* was a highwayman. Noun and verb are definitely cant. *Win*, to steal, is almost certainly cant, and it appears as such at the end of the seventeenth century in B.E.'s dictionary ; Grose also gives it.

II. FOOD ; TERMS OF ADDRESS ; IMPRISONMENT ; THE INFANTRY AND THEIR GROUSING

Some of the best-known Army slang words concern food ; old friends like *pahny*, *rooty*, and the other Anglo-Indians, are hardly old enough to be admitted here. Whether *pozzy* merits inclusion is an open point. This frequently used word for jam is a mystery : for though it was certainly in use by 1884 (before jam became an article of ration issue) and began its English career as a Regular Army word, we do not know its age. Nor its origin. It comes from neither Hindustani nor Arabic (the two most fertile foreign sources of Regular Army slang). Some of the most knowledgeable people suggest a West Indian origin : others that it is from a South African language.[1] Very tentatively I suggest *posset*, by a corruption of spelling and a diversion of the meaning ; or rather, I suggest that an English-

[1] An old soldier at the Royal Hospital, Chelsea, says that *pozzy* was used, by South African natives in talking to soldiers, to signify any sort of sweetmeat or preserve. I owe this information to Brig.-General A. P. Wavell, C.M.G., M.C.

SLANG WITH A PAST

man, hearing a native word for some mixture resembling either a very thick, sweet posset or a thin, watery jam, applied the name *posset* and that, conscious of the twisted meaning of a good old word, those who used *posset* for near-jam, then by a natural transition for jam, sympathetically debased the form of the word. I put forward that purely semantic theory in the hope that someone who really does know will come forward and solve the problem : as we used to say in the Army, ' I'll be the mug.' With *burgoo* (often corrupted to *burgue*), porridge, we are on safer ground. Curiously enough, the word was, in dialect, obsolete before 1897, but it survived in the Regular Army and had a very vigorous life in 1914–18. Weekley records the probably artificial spelling *burgout* (gallomonia this !) in 1743 ; the O.E.D. gives an instance of *burgoo* in 1750. It was at first a sailors' word, the O.E.D. preferring not to risk an etymology, Weekley being cautious with ' ? Arab *burghul*, wheat dried and boiled ' ; Mr. T. E. Shaw (to give his less famous name) says : ' from *burghul*, Turkish and Arabic for wheat-porridge '. *Jippo* was meat-juice (especially bacon-fat or gravy) and occasionally butter. As nautical slang in 1870, *jipper* denoted gravy ; *bread and jipper*, bread and dripping ; and *jipper* as verb, to baste a bird or joint of meat. In London and the Isle of Wight, in 1902, it could mean the juice or the syrup of a pie, a pudding. In the modern form *jippo* or *gippo*, it is ignored by the O.E.D. The nearest that I can get to an etymology is *gippo*, a scullion (seventeenth-eighteenth century) ; and that is frankly a guess, although the transition from a scullion to a ' constant culinary feature ' needs only to be authenticated to be declared obvious. But it is more likely that the original form was *jipper*, a nautical word picked up one knows not where, and that the *gippo-jippo* form is due to the frequent use of *gyppo* (*gippo*), *jippo*, as variants of *gyppy*, *gippy*, *gippie* for an Egyptian. The general word for food was *scran*, employed also to designate a meal. Messrs. Fraser and Gibbons in ' Soldier and Sailor Words and Phrases ', 1925, say that it was a Navy word, and Frank C. Bowen (op. cit.) tersely defines thus : ' *Scran. Naval food.*' The word certainly dates back in the Regular Army, however, to about 1860 : several staff officers have written to say that they think the Army used it considerably before that year. Weekley suggests that *scran* is cognate with *scrannel*, lean, meagre. Grose in his remarkable ' Vulgar Tongue ' (1785) simply says ' victuals '. The probable genesis is : refuse, broken victuals ; an impromptu meal ; food. *Scran-bag* was military slang for a haversack at least as early as 1864, as Hotten's Dictionary proves. *Tommy* was likewise used for food in general, but originally it meant bread ; it is a Regular Army word. *Brown George*, defined by Grose as ' an ammunition loaf ', arose in the previous century to designate a coarse brown loaf : there may possibly be a pun [1] suggested by *brown musket* (seventeenth century), *brown Bess* (eighteenth century). *Brown Tommy* is apparently a late eighteenth-century variation on *Brown George*, and it soon became alternatively *Tommy Brown*, then it shortened to *Tommy*, thence *tommy* ; as early as 1783, according to Cobbett, *tommy* signified brown bread ;

[1] Aided by the fact that *brown George* was, in the Navy, a name for bread supplied by contract and more ' officially ' known as Munition Bread.—Bowen (op. cit.).

at Chatham, he adds, white bread was just 'bread'. Grose, in 1788, glosses *tommy* thus : ' Soft Tommy, or white Tommy ; bread is so called by sailors to distinguish it from biscuit.' The word may, I think, be considered as common to both Services, despite the fact that Fraser and Gibbons (op. cit.) ignore it and Bowen says merely : ' soft bread '.

Of the various Army terms of address, *chum* and *cobber* are the most interesting. Among English troops, *chum* was slightly more popular than *mate* and much more popular than *pal*, while among the Australians *cobber* shared the honours with *digger* (from the early gold-rush days). *Chum* arose in the seventeenth century, when it designated intimates at the universities of Oxford and Cambridge : ' The Dictionary of the Canting Crew ' defines it as ' a chamber-fellow, or constant companion '. Originally quite good English, it rapidly degenerated ; Johnson has it ; Grose remarks : ' a chamber-fellow, particularly at the universities and in prison '. *Cobber* itself does not, I believe, date before 1890, and the absence of any definite clue in such authorities as the O.E.D., Farmer and Henley, and Morris rather frightened me, for I did not wish to hide behind ' apparently an obscure Australianism ', for this *cobber* has obviously nothing to do with *cobber*, a great lie (cf. a whopping or a rapping lie), nor with the Cornish *cobba*, a simpleton, a bungler, nor even with *cob* (originally Suffolk dialect), to take a liking to : actually it comes from the Hebrew and Yiddish *chaber*.

One said *to click for* something good, *to click* something bad, i.e. to come in for ; intransitively, *to click* meant to strike up a temporary acquaintance with a girl (who could likewise use the word). In eighteenth-century cant, *click* signified to snatch, whence came the sense, to seize, to catch.

Clicking with a girl might lead to the less pleasant acquaintance with the *cage, clink, jankers, jug,* or *quod,* all of which are adoptions from civilian ' low slang '. *Cage* dates from the late fifteenth century ; Shakespeare uses it in 1593 ; in the seventeenth century it was still good English ; Johnson defined it as ' a prison for petty malefactors ' ; soon after, it became slang ; by about 1850 it had reached the lowliest status of all, cant. In 1914–18, when so much of the lowest stratum of language came to the surface, it did duty for a barbed-wire enclosure for prisoners of war and, though this is loose and exceptional, for a prison. *Clink* was the guard-room when and as it held offenders prior to trial. As early as 1515, Barclay used it of the famous prison in Southwark ; thence (though the converse may have been true) it seems to have been applied to other prisons ; in respect of the converse we may note that Grose suggests as the origin : ' the clinking of prisoners' chains or fetters ', but another possibility is the old verb *clink,* to fasten securely. *Jankers*[1] meant primarily punishment cells, secondarily defaulters' punishment and even ' the Defaulters ', i.e. the defaulters' bugle-call. (Whence *the jankers king,* the provost sergeant.) I suspect the word of being very old, but I cannot prove this. As the obvious sources disclose no evidence, I conjecture a cant *janglers,* chains, corrupted to *jankers* partly because of the name, and the sense, of *clink*. *Jug,* either a military prison staffed by ' Red Caps ' or else a regimental

[1] In the Navy : defaulters.

guard-room, is the abbreviation of *stone-jug*,[1] which
first, according to certain authorities, occurs in 1834
in Harrison Ainsworth's ' Rookwood ' ; but Ainsworth
pillaged Grose at every turn : Grose in 1788 has
' *Stone Jug.* Newgate, or any other prison.—*Stone
Tavern.* Ditto ', two terms lacking in the 1st edition
(1785), which, however, has the variant *stone-doublet.*
All three terms belong to cant. *Quod*, ' perhaps
originally the quadrangle of the prison ' (Weekley),
is first recorded *c.* 1700 in the ' Dictionary of the Canting Crew ' : ' *Quod.* Newgate ; also any prison, tho'
for debt ' ; it may rather be connected with *qued, quad,*
bad, evil—a wicked person—the Devil—evil, harm.
In 1914-18 *quod* denoted either a military prison or
a term of imprisonment. *Clink, jug,* and *quod* were
also used as verbs signifying to imprison, the length
of the sentence having little to do with it except that
jug was the most serious and forbidding term. Even
the *lead-swinger* and the *column-dodger* sometimes found
himself in prison.

Swing the lead, to malinger, is a figurative use of the
old nautical term : the sailor thus engaged had an
excellent chance of ' taking things easy ' and of wast-
ing time. *Dodge the column* was a little more specific,
for it meant to avoid a dangerous or some otherwise
particularly unpleasant job ; the phrase, in use during the Boer War, probably originated during the
Peninsular War.

The true *foot-slogger* or infantryman did neither.
This term is comparatively modern, but its type is
found in Grose, who defines a *foot-wabler* (i.e. *foot-
wobbler*) as ' a contemptuous term for a foot soldier,

[1] Cf. the old Navy term *stone-frigate*, a naval gaol.

frequently used by those of the cavalry'. One heard also in 1914–18 the variants *gravel-grinder* (cf. the French *pousse-caillou*, a pebble-pusher), *beetle-crusher*, *mud-crusher* and *worm-crusher*; though these four terms were already current in the eighteen-nineties, I do not know just how much further back they go; *beetle-crusher*, however, is a development of the same term (variant: *beetle-squasher*) in the sense of a large, flat foot—'the expression', says Hotten, 'was made popular by being once used by Leech', and *mud-crusher* is recorded by Hotten as 'a word of contempt, used by the cavalry in reference to the infantry'; with this last, compare the eighteenth-century *officer of feet*, 'a jocular title for an officer of infantry'. The commonest German slang words for an infantryman (*Infanterist*) are *Dreckfresser* and *Kilometerfresser*, mud- and kilometre-glutton; *Fusslatsche*, foot-shuffler, cf. Grose's *foot-wabler*; *Kilometerschwein*; *Lakenpatscher*, something like our *mud-crusher*; and *Sandhase*, literally sand-hare (i.e. in literary German, white hare).

The best of soldiers considered that they had a right to *grouse*, a word used by Kipling in 1892. Professor Weekley, contrary to the O.E.D., thinks it 'impossible to link the military *grouse* [1] with old French *groucier*, as there is a gap of centuries between them'; this is not to imply that there is no connexion, for the 'missing links' will probably be found, perhaps in such words as *grudge* and the American *grouch*. The Naval equivalents of *grouse* as noun are *bleat* and *moan*. The worst *grouse* sometimes came from the soldier with the most *guts*, the germ-sense of which is 'substance'

[1] Redding Ware, op. cit., says, in 1912, 'This is a provincial word still in extensive use for worrying and scratching.'

as in *to have guts in one's brain,* as used by Butler in 1663 and Swift somewhat later. But any kind of soldier liked *jam on it,* i.e. something pleasant, a luxury, surplus, unexpected windfall. *All jam,* at least as early as 1882—*real jam* in ' Punch ', 1885—and *jam and fritters* in Mary Kingsley, 1895, all meaning ' a real treat ', are probable parents, while an ancestor is to be found in the adjective *sweet,* defined by Grose as ' easy to be imposed on, or taken in ; also expert, dexterous, clever '.

III. OLD SOLDIERS, THEIR TRIALS AND BATTLES ; ' TOMMY ATKINS ' AND HIS DYING

Kamerad, literally comrade, is the famous German entreaty for mercy.[1] The word itself has a strong literary flavour, as we see, for example, in Grose's definition of a *camerade* : ' A chamber fellow ; a Spanish military term. Soldiers were in that country divided into chambers, five men making a chamber, whence it was generally used to signify companion.' Analogous to the French *chambrée,* a military mess or a barrack-room.

Kip meant to sleep ; also a bed, any place in which to sleep, and sleep itself.[2] Probably the word was originally thieves' slang ; the O.E.D. gives ' a common lodging-house ; also a lodging or bed in such a house ; hence, a bed in general ', and says that the origin is uncertain, but Weekley appears to have solved the difficulty by finding the etymology in the Danish *kippe,*

[1] In surrendering to French soldiers, the Germans would say : *Kamarade, pas kapout.*—François Déchelette, ' L'Argot des Poilus ', 1918.
[2] In nautical slang, a hammock, bunk or sleep.—Bowen, op. cit.

a mean hut, an alehouse. The soldier's *pack* was more properly called valise, officially knapsack, and, in its other sense, his full equipment : the second meaning has been influenced by the connotation, a heap or lot of things, dating from Shakespeare ; the former derives from a *pedlar's pack*, and, by itself, it may be found in Spenser's ' Shepherd's Calendar '.

If the soldier's kip were notably dirty, or his pack just perceptibly irregular, the sergeant-major (*the Major*), who would be sure to have him *taped*, would speak to some purpose. Occasionally tapes were laid in the open to indicate the ' jump-off ' of an attack : hence ' Jerry has got us taped ' signified that the Germans had the exact range ; while ' the S.M. has that bleeder taped ' implied a fear that some ranker was unfavourably sized-up by that important person. After disposing of the offender, the S.M. might be glad to go to *Wypers*, a pronunciation of Ypres encouraged by the powers at the very beginning of the War, perhaps as a reminiscence of the Ypre Tower (locally Wypers) at Rye, the old Cinque port that naturally had close business relations with Flanders. The surnames *Wiper* and *Wypers* also represent Ypres, as, though less obviously, do *Diaper* and *Dipper*, John de Ipre occurring in documents of *c.* 1200, as Professor Weekley mentions in his ' Surnames '.

Two phrases much heard in 1917-18 were *old soldier* and *old sweat*, the latter probably denoting a Regular Army man, the former a soldier (whether a Regular or not) who carried his experience to the point of cunning and his cunning to the verge of malingering. *Old soldier*, printed as a verb in 1892, has not caught on ; it is an embroidering of *Come the old soldier over*, which we find in Scott's 'St. Ronan's Well', 1824. *To soldier*, usually in the form *soger*, is in Dana's 'Two Years before the Mast', 1840, in the sense of malinger, shirk one's job, and it has remained a nautical term to this day : Bowen defines *sogering* as ' loafing, acting like a soldier on shipboard '. The same authority records *soldier* as a term of contempt applied to any inferior seaman, a *soldier's mast* for a pole mast without sails, *soldier-walking* for any land operations carried out by bluejackets ; while Grose has *soldier's bottle*, a large one, and *soldier's pomatum*, a piece of tallow candle. *An old soldier* is now synonymous with a shirker, a malingerer, or an ' artful dodger '.

Over the top the soldier, however ' old ', had to go if he belonged to the infantry ; the phrase, varied to *over the bags*, may be compared with the old-warfare *into the breach*, i.e. enter the gap made by a battery in the enemy's fortification. (*To stand in the breach* was the defender's part ; both phrases became metaphors.) As the man *hopped the bags*, he hoped that this would be a good *show*, by which he would understand an attack, a raid. *Show* often meant a bombardment or a local engagement, *push* connoting an attack on a wide front. *Push* was employed in a frontal instead of a lateral sense by Napier in his ' Peninsular War ', 1828 : ' making a " push " of 400 miles ' ; by Napier's day *push* had become obsolete in its early military meaning of an attack or vigorous onset, as in Golding's translation of Caesar, 1563, and in Earl Orrery's ' Art of War ', 1677. The history of *show* is not so clear. As ' a demonstration or display of military strength or of intention to take severe measures ', to quote the O.E.D. definition, the word has persisted from the middle of the sixteenth century. This meaning is linked up with that of a 'display on a large scale', which we see in such a statement as 'the battalion put up a damned good show'. Those who returned from a successful attack would hope for, and do their best to *wangle*, leave. *Wangle* is modern, 1888 being the first 'printed' date; the origin is obscure, but the word was probably by *new-fangled* out of *waggle*.

The French soldiers' slang is as vivid as our own. Indeed the *poilu* was a smart fellow, and his nickname was known to many. *Poilu* was used of a soldier by Balzac in 1834, the word dating back much further. Its history is in fact less disputed than that of the English *Tommy*, which everybody knows is short for *Tommy Atkins*, more formally *Thomas Atkins*. George Augustus Sala in 1883 spoke of 'Private Tommy Atkins, returning from Indian service', and Kipling of 'Tommy' in 1892. Like 'John and Richard Doe', and like the earlier 'John-a-Nokes' and 'Tom-a-Stiles' (who died of obsolescence about 1760), Thomas Atkins is a formal name; it was first used, probably quite casually, in the specimen forms given in the War Office's Orders and Regulations of 31 August 1815; and in the War of 1914–18, the Canadians had, in their pay-books, a specimen will with this name of *Thomas Atkins*. The eloquent 'story' by the late Lieut.-Colonel Newnham-Davis, writing for the Royal Society of St. George, is wrong about the date of the first official use of the name, but I am assured, by an eminent authority on military history, that there was an actual Thomas Atkins, who died in action in Holland in 1794 and that his commanding officer

SLANG WITH A PAST

was young Colonel Wellesley. 'He was', writes this correspondent, 'a member of the 33rd Regiment of Foot which is now the 1st Battalion of the Duke of Wellington's Regiment (West Riding). He stood six foot three and is possibly the source of *every inch a soldier*', on the analogy, one assumes, of Shakespeare's ' every inch a king ', ' Lear ', IV, vi. A much less significant word is *swaddy*, sometimes heard in 1914–18 as a term of address among soldiers, more often as meaning a private soldier. The eighteenth-century forms were *swadkin* and *swad-gill* with the basic or abbreviated *swad*; the first and the third of these are described by Grose as cant. But *swad*, soldier, was probably a development of the near-dialectal *swad*, a country bumpkin, a clodhopper, a loutish fellow or a clumsy and ignorant fellow, these senses being very rare indeed after the Restoration.

One of the most picturesque of War terms is *No Man's Land*. Originally it denoted waste ground, barren stretches between two kingdoms or provinces. An official Roll of the year 1320 contains *nonesmanneslond*; Defoe in 1719 writes it *no Man's Land*, T. Hughes in 1881 *noman's land*, Dilke in 1890 *no man's land*, ' The Month ' in 1892 *no-man's-land*: the O.E.D. prefers the uncapitalled *no man's land*.

It was in this area between the aligned trenches that many a man *copped a packet*, gave up his *cold-meat ticket*, *became a landowner* and began *to push up daisies*: where, in finer words, he *went west*. In *cop a packet*, *cop* (now slang) is probably a dialectal form of *cap*, the obsolete verb to seize, from old French *caper*, to seize, and *packet* often has, and long has had, the meaning of a packet of lies or something else that is unpleasant, as in *to sell someone a packet* ; *to cop a packet* probably began by indicating the reception of the unpleasantness ; at first in 1914–18 it connoted to be either wounded or killed, but it soon came to signify only the latter. A *cold-meat ticket* is one of those brutally cynical yet inherently courageous terms which characterized the Tommy's speech : it refers to his identity disc. It is formed on the analogy of *cold-meat box*, a coffin, itself an extension of *cold-meat*, a corpse, as in Tom Moore's slangy ' Tom Crib ', 1819. *To become a landowner* is to be dead and buried, the estate being the grave ; *a landowner in France* was often heard in place of ' Killed on the Western Front '. The metaphor is presumably old in its idea but modern in its phrasing. *To push up daisies* is a War-time phrase, but *to turn up one's toes to the daisies* [1] occurs in Barham's ' Ingoldsby Legends ', 1837. This figure for post-mortem burial and its finality was probably, in some form or other, coined before Barham's time. *To go west* in the seventeenth century described the passage of the condemned criminal from Newgate to Tyburn, where, in that part of London nowadays called Marylebone, stood the great gallows known as Tyburn Tree (Weekley, ' Adjectives and other Words ', 1930). This I believe to be the operative origin of the phrase, though romantic associations have enriched it and impregnated it with something of awe and suffused it with much of sentiment : the image of the sun setting in the west, the metaphor of the day there going to its death, as in the Greek proverb ὁ βίος ἕσπερον ἄγει (life draws towards its evening, the west, the setting

---

[1] Cf. the pre-War slang of British residents in India, *to grin at the daisy-roots*, and the more general *go to grass with one's teeth up*.

sun); and the journeying westwards of the pioneers in North America, the long trail that often led to peril and death. The metaphor began in English literature at the beginning of the fifteenth century ('it was night, the sun goeth west'), in the sixteenth it gathered force with its transference to human beings ('55 women . . . are gone west'), in the seventeenth and eighteenth centuries it gained an admixture of violence (death by hanging), in the nineteenth the Americans revived the phrase, and in the twentieth century we have seen too many of our friends and our people meet their death like a gallant sun dipping over the western horizon that a better day might be born : westering to the dark that light might come.

GERMAN ARMY SLANG: A NOTE [1]

NOW that the tumult and the shouting dies, now that the hysteria of the ' national ' newspapers is viewed askance, now that the latrine War books, on the one hand, and the Angels of Mons type of absurdity, on the other, are fast becoming discredited and have, indeed, been dismissed as ' stunts ', we can talk of the long and deadly struggle of 1914–18 with something like equanimity. We do not necessarily believe a writer on War politics because he happens to have held a too prominent position during those critical years, we do not deferentially accept a General's tirade as gospel truth, nor, at the opposite extreme, do we give much weight to the internationalist bestiality of a private possessing no more than a cleverly tricked out knowledge gleaned in a hospital from weary soldiers recently come from the Front Line (*Schützengraben*, the ' Shooting-Gallery ' of the Tommy), or to the artistic and mediumistic reconstruction by a man that was not ' there ' at all. We can think kindly of our foes, whether ' the gallant dead ' or the no less gallant living. Only perverters of the public mind now speak glibly of ' the horrid

---

[1] This essay is unintentionally very much shorter than that which precedes and that which follows it. But German is given equal importance with the French and English in the comparative study on the soldiers' slang of these three nations.

GERMAN ARMY SLANG

Hun' and fail to remember that almost every British soldier can attest the humanity and thoughtfulness, as he must vividly recall the fortitude, of the German soldier, while the quiet heroism and the willingness to 'carry on' of the German civilian have not yet been adequately described to the English public. All this may now be recognized without more than a few arm-chair patriots or cast-iron professional soldiers raising a cry of treachery or bringing an indignant charge of blind Germanophilism.

Public opinion would be still more humanized if it could be made to comprehend the courage, the resourcefulness, the humour, and the hatred of hypocrisy displayed by the German common soldier. One of the best ways to understand these qualities is to study the slang of the men in question. That slang necessarily depends for its basic characteristics on the genius of the German language. Without analysing all life out of that arresting entity, German soldiers' slang, one can note a few of the constant and powerful factors that go to make it what it is; its compounds, picturesque at their best and ponderously unwieldy at their worst; realistic vividness, conveying a picture sometimes Dutch in its faithfulness and sometimes brilliant in its impressionism; a materialism that is either trenchantly despondent or equably comfortable; a grossness sometimes Rabelaisian; a droll humour, either puckish or generous; a cynicism that may be sly and good-humoured, or direct and terrible, the latter characteristic being understandably prominent if we consider all that the German N.C.O. and private had to tolerate and endure; and the malicious or the dryly humorous sarcasms and ironies directed at officers.

It is perhaps explainable by the national characters concerned that while the French had published three excellent dictionaries of their soldiers' slang before July 1919, the Germans published no thoroughly satisfactory one on theirs till 1925, the year in which appeared the valuable book of Messrs. Fraser and Gibbons, the first on our own soldiers' slang. The French have, I believe, issued nothing of note on the subject since 1919, the Germans nothing since 1925, the English nothing more till 1930. The German glossary, ' Schwere Brocken ', is extremely business-like in its brief definitions. By Sigmund Graff (author of ' Meine Fresse ') and Walter Bormann, it is pertinently and humorously illustrated by Eduard Thöny. It contains nearly 3,000 slang words ; a number of short sections illuminatingly grouped for the civilian reader ; and a list of such sayings as were popular with the soldier, especially the front-liner. It is a valuable volume and, after the authors are dead, their labours will be fully incorporated in some great dictionary of colloquial German. It is, moreover, a work that should help to dispel the almost complete ignorance of the British and the Americans with regard to the speech of the gallant foe in those ' hectic ' years.

The various classes of soldier are for the most part aptly named. An infantryman was a *mud-eater, mile-eater, mile-pig, Indian with sweaty feet (Schweissfussindianer), foot-shuffler, puddle-splasher* ; if in the trenches, a *Front-pig, -sow, -ox,* or *-bull*. The far-famed Jäger was variously called a *grasshopper, cockchafer, tree-frog, quack-quack*. The Hussar was a *Death's head*, a *pack-thread* or *straps-youth* (from the lacings and facings) ; if a

Red Hussar, a *glow-worm*. The lowly Pioneer got such names as *earth-rat* and *mole* (to attempt to distinguish between the synonymous *Erdratte* and *Maulwurf*), *pick-axe, ram-buck* (note the pun). One debased the magnificent Cavalryman to a *sack-rider, sole-preserver, mud-stamper, horse-onion shaker*, while the now ' legendary ' Uhlan became a mere *wooden-head, toad-spitter* or *-sticker*, and, on account of his lance, a *lamp-lighter*. The Artillery was, by abbreviation, *Ari* or, playfully, *Young Barbara*, a gunner a *field* or *common hare, field-banger, postman*, or generically *Ernest*[1] ; a Trench Mortar man, a *footer, boomer* (boom !). A telegraphist (one of the specialists among the very versatile German signallers) was generally known as a *string-puller, T-carrier* (from the *T* on his shoulder-straps), *semicolon-strategist* ; a Telephonist, with poignantly brief reference to his many trials and troubles, a *wirer*. The Cyclist Company aptly moved as *the tossing brigade*, a member thereof as a *wire-donkey rider*. Those lucky enough to belong to the Band were derisively called *tin-puffers* or *-blowers*, even *verdigris-spitters*. And Recruits, no matter which arm of the Service might claim them, were *greenies, callow boys, greenhorns, wethers* or *bell-wethers, dung-beetles*, and—worse. The close examination of such a group of words will make one suspect what one soon finds to be correct. German Army slang is wonderfully rich in substantival synonyms, but it is so much poorer than English in synonyms for verbs and adjectives that we may without distortion restrict ourselves to the nouns.

Some of the slang names for Non-Commissioned

[1] Just as the infantryman was generically *Fritz* or *Otto*, and the aviator *Franz* (whence *sich verfranzen*, to get lost).

Officers and Officers are significant. An N.C.O. was a *spider* or *uniform-stallion*, a Corporal an *over-bull*, a Sergeant a *joker*, a Company Sergeant-Major a *fat of the meat, cousin, churl, company-mother, bidder to a funeral*, a Regimental Sergeant-Major a *half-and-half* (neither N.C.O. nor Officer), *bastard-lieutenant, lieutenant lance-corporal, C.S.M.'s corpse*. A Second Lieutenant was a *star-gazer*, a First Lieutenant a *senior master*. A Captain, a Major, a Lieutenant-Colonel, and (as in the British forces) a Colonel were all called *the old man*, but if a Captain (his horse, by the way, was a *battle-donkey*) were one of the four Company Commanders, he completed *the four knaves*, and the Major, Lieutenant-Colonel, and the Colonel were additionally known as *God Almighty* and *maggot-breeder*, the latter being a pun on the double sense of *Raupen*, maggots (and their like) and those thick fringes on epaulettes which distinguished the higher officers. An Adjutant was *the battalion Aunt, chief clerk, maid of all work, kaleidoscope*. A Staff-Officer perhaps deserved, or rather would have been glad always to deserve, the envious name of *brandy-officer*. A Chaplain had about forty nicknames, none complimentary and some very blasphemous.

The list of slang terms for various garments and parts of equipment is too rich to be treated as it merits, but certain of the argotic acrobatics and aptnesses cannot be dismissed thus cavalierly. *Louse-catcher* was a shirt, *banana-case* a stocking, *ventilator* a cloak, *gondola* or *dice-box* or *child's coffin* a boot, *corset* or *life-belt* or *stomach-reducer* (likewise *belly-brake* and *tummy-tamer*) a belt, *percussion-cap* a service cap, *battle-hat* or *tulip of the storm* a steel helmet, *Hugo* or *back-*

GERMAN ARMY SLANG

warmer or *chest of drawers* or *Regulation marching-box* a knapsack, *bee-hive* a cholera-belt (*Bienenkorb*, bees in German slang being lice), *tea-* or *coffee-spoon* a spade, *thistle-pricker* or *jack-knife* or (as in English) *tooth-pick* a bayonet, *Laura* or *syringe* or *lath* or *rattle* or *bride* or *crowbar* or *Brown Bess* (the last three current in Army slang since 1900 or earlier) a rifle.

The names for the more deadly weapons and their missiles are numerous; we select the machine-gun and the (artillery) shell. For the former we have such picturesqueries as *barrel-organ, stuttering aunt* and *fairy*, the *tack-tack, ma'm'selle of the dots* (*Tippmamsell*; with the mongrelism, compare *der Herr du jour*, the orderly officer), *bean-* and *ball-sprinkler* (the latter a survival from the Franco-Prussian War), the *slater* or *tiler*, *revolver-nozzle*, and *mincing-machine*. For the latter: *big bit, flower-pot, attaché-case* and *sample box, gift* or *comfort, truck, furniture van*, and *councillor*, the last three of the larger shells. Those other annoyances, lice, were variously condemned as *foreign trade, deserters, blind passengers, sneaks, mess-mates, secret patrol*, and *Russians*: they were troublesome in billet and a perfect plague in dug-out; the latter, by the way, was styled the *onion* (and *the heroes'*) *cellar, U-boat, smoking-compartment,* and *grotto*. With the vivid vocabulary pertaining to the Air Force and the Army Service Corps I feel incompetent to deal.

Food evoked many synonyms. 'Bread was the principal food', and its slang name *Karo* presumably came from cards; *Karo* being carreau, a diamond: query, 'hard as diamonds'. Over numerous graphic terms we must pass in favour of the prolific marmalade: *army fat* and *tonic, athlete's grease* and *mixture, hero-fat*, *Hindenburg's cream* and *Ludendorff's bounty* and *Kaiser Wilhelm's remembrance butter*, *listening-post's dripping*, *infantryman's impulse*, *life-prolonging grease*, *army-bread rouge*, *tonic* and *cream* and *pap* (&c. &c.) *for the offensive*.

A cigarette was neatly named *monkey-flute*, *churchyard asparagus*, *pendulum*, and, as in English, *coffin-nail*, while a cigar merited *stink-* and *refreshment-peg*, *broom*, *coat-hanger*, *fly-killer* and *fly-killer paste*, *poison-wisp*, *gas-attack*, *holiday carrot*, *Field Grey*, and *glimmer-stick*, this last dating from at least as early as 1900. Special names were given to various kinds of cigar, such as *railway signal-man*, ' out at every puff ' ; *reporter*, ' carbonizes (i.e. gasses) frightfully ' ; *cheerfulness* ; *too crooked glimmer*, ' the longer it glows, the more obliquely it burns ' ; *group-leader* or *corporal*, ' has no sympathy ' ; *hand-grenade*, ' to be sent, to be thrown away ' ; *Wild Rose*, ' and the rude boy plucked [it] ', a quotation from Goethe's famous poem, ' Heideröslein ' ; *Hercules*, ' only a strong man can smoke one ' ; *Kaiser Frederick*, ' learn to suffer without complaining ', a clever allusion ; *female cook*, ' will go on for ever ' ; *a quarter's warning* or *notice*, ' it may draw then ' ; *Peter*, ' . . . went forth (i.e. out) and wept bitterly ' ; *chess-problem*, ' after three moves, mate ', with a pun signifying ' after three puffs, done for ' ; *Schiller's Bell*, ' the man must go forth ' (quotation punning ' out ') ; *King of the Elves*, ' obtains justice with trouble and pains ' (a quotation from a famous old poem) ; and *longing*, ' only he who knows it, knows what I suffer '.

This last group of words will, for apposite allusiveness and inevitability, bear comparison with anything in English or French soldiers' slang. Though

'Schwere Brocken' offers nothing else quite so attractive to the cultured, yet it has much of the vigour and the picturesqueness that have here been indicated only thus cursorily.

THE SLANG OF THE *POILU*[1]

THE French had three excellent glossaries of the Poilu's slang by June 1919 : six years before either the Germans or the English published an adequate dictionary for Fritz and Tommy.

All three French lexicographers claim to have completed their work before the end of the War, but, while that claim is correct, we must make the order of merit depend, in some degree at least, on the order of publication. François Déchelette's ' L'Argot des Poilus ' appeared in the autumn of 1918 ; almost immediately after, came Albert Dauzat's ' L'Argot de la Guerre ', in the second edition of which (early 1919) we find such a reference to Déchelette as renders him far less than justice ; and in the spring of 1919 Gaston Esnault, utilizing both the others but not having seen Dauzat's second edition, brought out his ' Le Poilu tel qu'il se parle '.

With any one of these dictionaries a satisfactory knowledge of the French soldier's slang could be obtained, but for a thoroughly representative account recourse must be had to all three ; for a sound but not an exhaustive idea, Déchelette plus either of the others will suffice ; the truest notion of the War in general and of Poilu slang in particular is undoubtedly the debonair Déchelette's. Dauzat, the best philo-

[1] See also Appendix III.

logist, is well known outside France for his publications on language, wherein he combines a pleasant, leisurely style with a sound and versatile erudition. In ' L'Argot de la Guerre ', which takes no count of the year 1918, he gives about 1,640 entries in the glossary, which is very terse, brief, efficient, but of these words he notes that 330 were current in pre-War Parisian slang; perhaps even more valuable is that fascinating and important study of the influence of the War on, and its relation to, the French language which runs to about 38,000 words. Esnault thus characterizes Dauzat's work : ' It condenses, according to the best linguistic discipline, the results of an investigation conducted on perfect lines.' The manner of Dauzat's introductory essay may be gauged from the following short passage : ' Literary coinings are not in favour with the combatants, who nevertheless come to adopt them, along with many other words borrowed by the Front from the Rear.

' The best example is the celebrated *Rosalie* (bayonet), which has a habit of irritating numerous Poilus. As to the origin of the word there is no doubt : it was created by the song-writer Theodore Botrel, who wished to make a pendant to the ancient Durandal and who launched the word in a song published in " Le Bulletin des Armées " on 4 November 1914. The word's success with civilians restrained its propagation on many a sector of the front line. Yet—if its detractors will allow me to say so—it has prospered, for it was of a good mint and followed a tendency well known in every Western " language of the people " . . .

' *Bluets*, fathered by Lucien Descaves in " Le

Journal" in January 1916, to designate the young recruits of the 1917 class, proved much less popular.'

Whereas Dauzat, over military age, served actively for a few months in 1914, Déchelette had a long and honourable record at the front. After a brief but very interesting introduction (notably prefaced by G. Lenôtre), he proceeds to his 'dictionnaire humoristique et philologique', containing some 1,110 entries, many of which gave rise to an essay in little. Esnault characterizes it as 'vécu', and that is one of its charms: moreover, it is full of wit and good humour. Déchelette was learned too, though with a philological basis slightly less solid than that of Dauzat and Esnault; and he possessed a more alert intellect, a much more agreeable style, and a vastly more fluent procedure: like the dictionaries of Dr. Johnson, Professor Weekley and the Fowlers, 'L'Argot des Poilus' can be read with a pleasure that perhaps one does not expect from such works. His 'essay' on *gau* is wholly delightful, but its subject (lice) rather stands in its way here. More 'accessible' is the remark that follows his definition of *ficelle* as an officer's stripe: 'In civil life one is sometimes at a loss to know how, between two speakers, one is to distinguish which is right and which is wrong. In the Army it is quite simple: one has but to count the stripes; the one with the greater number is right. This evident truth saves much waste of time.'

Esnault, of an age midway between those of Dauzat and Déchelette, is more erudite than the latter, equally erudite with the former; he writes less well than either. His introduction is learned, though not particularly interesting, but his glossary (some 1,110 entries) is equally comprehensive with Déchelette's in number and much more so in treatment ; in addition to the entry-words, about 700 others are defined in the course, or at the end, of main notices (i.e. of the key or original words). If he sometimes errs by using too profusely the jargon of philology and by favouring a too erudite style, he is the frankest of the three and not merely cites but comments on words omitted by the other two glossarists ; also he lists some soldiers' sayings. To give a just idea of his manner, one is bound to quote in French : ' *baoulier*, m., Homme de corvée pour aller chercher le repas aux cuisines ; [cité par des] fantassins, secteurs de l'Aisne, mai [19]18.—*baoule*, f., Marmite, Chaudron ; ib.—Originaire de la région de Dinan et Pleurtuit, Le Bars, jeune fantassin témoin de ce mot, voit en *baoule* du patois de l'Aisne ; mais son régiment comptait nombre de Vendéens ; or, au Croisic, [19]12–14, la *baoule* est le Panier que porte à dos le pêcheur à crevettes ; en espagnol *baoul*, m., Colis. Plus lointain est *bouille*, *boille*, Récipient pour transporter le lait à la ville, en Jura suisse.' Esnault, in short, is a joy to scholars . . . but he is ' hard going ' for the man in the street ; by the ordinary public, indeed, only Déchelette will be read with pleasure.

For general observations on Poilu slang, however, Dauzat is the best : to him I owe the facts, and if not the facts at least the prompting, of the following introductory remarks, but first I must note three short passages in Esnault's and Déchelette's introductions. The former pointedly says : ' A word is Poilu either by the object designated or by its intensive use. Poilu the words created by the soldier to describe the fighting; but Poilu also are certain synonyms for To Eat, Drink, Fast, Die, Quarrel, Toil, because these are a fighter's dominant ideas.' Déchelette not only points out the extraordinary number of synonyms (it is with groups of synonyms, not with scattered words, that I shall concern myself when I reach examples of 'Poilu') but postulates the following important data in a passage freely translated thus: 'The isolated existence of a group of men, the communion of sentiment and feeling, and occupations in common form the ideal conditions for the birth of a slang. If one considers the chasm separating the Poilu from the civilian in his manner of feeling and in his daily tasks; if one remembers that in the first two or three months of the War the Poilus lived—and died—in almost complete isolation: then one will not be astonished at the rise of " Poilu ".

'What a multitude of new things, actions, and sensations to describe: what a dearth of ready-made words! The Poilu coined words for the new facts and enriched old words for changed conditions; he gave a new meaning to words from ancient or modern slang, from dialect or from standard French. . . .

'When the War became more or less static, became in short trench-warfare, the soldiers' slang grew and spread. Reliefs of one unit by another, like the movements of troops from one sector to another, helped to generalize words hitherto used only by small groups of men.'

Now to excerpt the most important of Dauzat's remarks on 'Poilu': not blindly, but in the light of my own experience in Egypt and Gallipoli and on the Western Front, and with frequent side-glances at

THE SLANG OF THE *POILU*

Esnault and Déchelette. Having noted that during the last twelve months of the War the various specialized slangs, e.g. that of the Air Force, were fusing rapidly with the general stock and that, of this period one might almost say that there was a definite Poilu slang common to all, Dauzat speaks illuminatingly on the four chief sources of this military slang : the influence of the French Colonial troops and of the many foreign soldiers that fought on the Western Front ; that of the German occupation of the North of France ; of the French corps in Gallipoli, Salonika, and Italy ; and of the prisoners in Germany—much the least important. These sources, taken in mass, produced perhaps fewer Poilu terms than those which came, separately, from any one of : Parisian slang transformed ; the pre-War vocabulary of the barracks ; dialect ; or revivals and changes, metaphors and puns operated in the more or less normal French. The latter sources represent internal influence, always much stronger in a live and lively language than any external, i.e. virtually foreign, influences can be. The foreign words and phrases may seem to be more interesting than, but they are rarely so long-lived as, the congruous graftings on the domestic stock. The mixing of the classes is more potent than the mixing of the nations.

Old military slang is obviously a very important source : this comes from the Regular Army, as in England, but also from ' the barracks ', i.e. from those thousands who have performed their compulsory military service. When the latter were mobilized they proudly remembered themselves of the old barrack words. In barracks, too, it is notorious that the peasant adopts the expressions of the workman far more than the latter adopts dialect; nevertheless, when a number of country men are gathered together, they tend to preserve their dialect. Provincialisms are less numerous than either barrack or Parisian slang words. Some of the former date as far back as the sixteenth century, but the latter are the more important for the simple reason that the capital has always had much to say in the character of military slang. Moreover, as 'the lower classes' predominate in barracks, so it is rather their speech than that of the intellectuals which has determined the predominant element in military slang. While it is true that Poilu slang adopted many technical terms, which it usually twisted to its own rare purposes, the official language of the Army took over such Poilu words as *boche*, *sauter* ('jump to it'), *saucisse* (observation balloon), *poilu* [1] (man in the ranks), and *barda* (full equipment).

Before passing to borrowings from foreign languages, we may just record that perhaps the most famous Poilu words originating in the provinces are *gnôle* (or *niôle*), brandy; *bourrin*, a horse; *zigouiller*, to kill; and *pastis*, either boredom or some specific thing that is disagreeable. Italian gave few words, the most important being *pignate*, a shell, from *pignatta*, a saucepan; Spanish, *moukère*, a prostitute, already well known in Paris long before the War. Lingua franca was responsible for *malabar*, sly, or big and pretty; *bamboula*, a Negro, or a Sengalese sharp-shooter; *barda*; *barbaque*, meat, especially if bad; and *estanco*, a dug-out. German influence came either from prisoners of war (both Germans in France and French-

[1] See Appendix IV on this word.

THE SLANG OF THE *POILU* 169

men in Germany) or from previous knowledge of that language or from intercommunication : as in *estourbir*, to kill ; *schloff*, sleep or a bed ; *flingue*, a rifle ; *faire camarade*, to surrender, from *Kamerad !* ; *minenwerfer* ; *verboten*, *ersatz* (compensation), from French prisoners in Germany. Of the English words, some are anterior to the War ; *bizness*, work, affair ; *pouloper*, to gallop, from ' pull up ' ; from the vocabulary of boxing, both *souinger*, to bombard, from ' swing ', and *uppercut*, brandy ; a group meaning chic, smart, good, excellent, consists of *ridère*, from ' (gentleman) rider ', an English horseman being, as by legend, a capital, smart one— *bath*, especially in *c'est bath*, that's capital ! or It's tip-top ! (*c'est ridère* and *c'est palace* are exact equivalents), from Bath, a town celebrated for its elegance— *palace*, the English palace being traditionally comfortable and luxurious, hence *nous allons être palaces*, we're in for a cushy time ! Directly due to the War are *horse*, generally corrupted, no doubt deliberately, to *ours* ; *go*, that's all right ! *come on*, merely ' come ! ' ; *tanks*, *sops* (Sopwith 'planes) and *Tommies* ; *finish*, there's no more !, it's over now ! ; *sévère* as in *pertes sévères*, journalistic and very un-French ; *strafer*, to bombard, to ill-treat, from German originally but due wholly to Tommy usage ; *vaseux*, dreamy and irresolute, from a fusion of ' muddy ' and ' muddled ' ; *coltar* (coal tar), wine ; *afnaf*, either not too well pleased or satisfied, or else exhausted, from ' half and half ' ; *olrède*, excellent, perfect, from ' all right ' ; *lorry* with plural *lorrys*. From Arabic we have *faire la nouba*, to go on the spree, to have a good time (pre-War) ; *clebs* or *cleps*, since 1900 for a dog, since 1914 for a corporal ; *caoua*, since 1888 for coffee ; *toubib*, since 1870 for medical officer ; *bled*, no man's land ; *guitoune* and *gourbi*, dug-out, though in the original the former meant a tent, the latter an earth-built house ; *cabir*, captain ; *kébour*, cap. From Annamite came *cagna*, the most popular of all names for a dug-out.

Among changes in the sense of the ordinary 'standard' and of popular slang words we find terms due to many causes. Facetiousness engendered *machine à coudre*, *machine à secouer le paletot*, machine-gun ; *mitrailleuse à haricots*, field kitchen ; *périscopes*, eyes ; *frigorifiés*, of frost-bitten feet ; *mies de pain mécaniques*, lice. Play on words is seen in *épilé*, a man with an easy job—prompted by *poilu*, 'the hairy one', soldier ; *beurre*, a man, a *type*, from the widely known trade-slogan, *le Tip remplace le beurre* ; in Salonika and the Dardanelles, *highlanders* were peas, *petits pois* High-landers, because both were *écossés*, *Ecossais*, perhaps the cleverest of the more brilliant among Poilu puns. By a different process a large nose is *coupe-vent*, macar-oni *kilomètre*, a bayonet *cure-dents*, *perle* a shell. The abstract, as indeed in all slang, becomes material, the material becomes brutal : equipment, for example, is *harnais*. Pejorative irony extends particularly to food, articles of clothing, officers, animals. Instances of forcible and picturesque grossness cannot be given in translation (such as *gros-cul* for canteen tobacco), nor of the acts and facts designated euphemistically by such a phrase as *téléphoner à Guillaume*.

Passing by the numerous graphic instances of meta-phor and simile, metonymy and synecdoche, we come to that very interesting class of slang words : proper names. *Jean le Gouin* represents the sailor, *Julot* either the gunner serving the French 75 or the cannon itself,

Fritz (in addition to being the German soldier in general) the German machine-gun or -gunner;[1] *Oscar* the rifle, *Joséphine* and *Rosalie* the bayonet, *Marguerite* a woman, *Bénard* (from Bernard) a pair of trousers, *Marie-Jeanne* a canteen. Well-known business firms have lent their names or their trade-marks to the fantasy of the Poilu. *Bergougnan*, the mark of a motor-tyre, is used for tough meat; so too is *Bibendum*, from the Pneu Michelin's pre-War (and post-War) advertisement, which shows a big man made up of motor-tyres. Material questions such as food and drink occupied much of the time and the thoughts of the soldier.

All such characteristics appear again and again in the following groups of synonyms, which have been selected from numerous starry clusters of verbal aptness and ingenuity. For the most famous of all French weapons, the cannon of 75 millimetres calibre (roughly equivalent to 3 inches, which, by the way, is the calibre of the British 18-pounder), we have already noticed the name of *Julot*. Other proper names are *Charlotte* and *Joséphine* (the latter also, as noted, a bayonet); semi-proper, *le petit Français*; patriotic, *le glorieux*; macabre, *râleur*; humorous, *bébé* and *roquet* (pug-dog or puppy); euphemistic, *coucou*; descriptive, *mirliton* (a reed-pipe), *pétard, zinzin*; and *tacot* (colloquially, a nail), which in Poilu slang also did duty for an engine, a taxi-cab, a supplies-train, an airman, a dirigible, an observation-balloon, a tank (locomotively belligerent), a typewriting machine, and a machine-gun, and is thus one of the three or four most fertile words in the whole range of the Poilu vocabulary.

[1] Contrast the German usage.

The machine-gun likewise has some picturesque names. In addition to *tacot*, we note *machine*, less popular by itself than in such compounds as *machine à signer les permissions*; *machine à broder les pans de capote* (i.e. for embroidering the skirts of a greatcoat), of which Esnault says with a peculiarly Gallic cynicism, 'it embroiders them in open-work, in scalloping and in lace'; whence *machine à coudre les pans de capote*, by confusion with, or as a development from, *machine à coudre*, a more usual term with the later *machine à dé coudre*, which is 'the contamination of the idea that the machine-gun unsews many of the enemy by the aural image of its "tac tac"' (Esnault); *machine à dépeupler*; *machine à ramer le paletot*, literally one that stretches the greatcoat on a frame, interpretatively 'one that lays the coat, and the man within it, upon the surface of no man's land'; rather more genially, *machine à secouer le paletot*, greatcoat-shaking machine, and its natural abridgement *secoue-paletot*; much the same idea apparently informs *machine à épousseter le paletot*, which is, however, due rather to the noise than to the process. But there are many others, such as *bécane*, literally a bicycle; *marouille*, of uncertain gender and infrequent use; *pétard à fesses*, *pétoche*, and *péteuse*; *poule*, from the laying of eggs; *bec-bois*, woodpecker in the dialect of Lorraine; *bousin*, masculine, and feminine; *crécelle*, a rattle, *arrosoir*, *écremeuse*, a skimmer; *grêle-à-mort*, rather journalistic than truly Poilu and perhaps rather a fancy name for a given machine-gun; *moulin à café*, a very general and popular term, wherein the similitude is not to the turning of a handle but partly to the dry rattling noise common to both instruments and even more to the rapid repetition of movement. Related are *moulin à poivre* and *poivrière*, pepper-mill and -pot ; *moulin à rata*, one apt to fail, to jamb, *rata* being a sub-French pun on both *(coup)raté* and *rateur* ; and by a hypothetical *moulin à turbutine* we reach *turbutine*, literally crushed biscuit, which, with the admixture of rice and bacon, was an active-service dish at least as early as the Crimean War.

More peaceful, but not less vigorous, is the set of names for meat, especially if either tough or, in any other way, not quite up to expectations. *Autobus*, fusing *automobile* and *omnibus*, is for meat so tough that not the best of jawbones could make any appreciable impression on it, the idea deriving not from the motor-conveyances of meat, as at least one great etymologist thought, but from the rubber-tyre consistency of the flesh. Of exactly the same implication and of the same or similar origin, are *rognure de taxis*, taxi-leavings or -parings ; *pneu*, short for *pneumatique de taxi* or *d'omnibus* ; *bergougnan*, *michelin*, *bibendum*, from Bergougnan and Michelin tyres, the third term relating to the latter manufacturer ; *viande blindée*, ' armoured ' meat ; and *élastique*. *Bidoche*, however, was meat either tolerable or good ; *dure* unexpectedly did not at all necessarily mean tough meat, for Barbusse and others have such phrases as *de la dure*, *bouillie* ; by lax development, *dure* was soup, presumably by transition from meat-soup.

Preserved, i.e. tinned meat, was called *boîte à grimaces*, which sometimes varied to *barbaque à la grimace* ; *barbaque* being the most popular of all trench names for meat, well known during the Franco-Prussian War, having originally a neutral sense but soon deteriorating to the pejorative, belonging chiefly to thieves' slang, and perhaps deriving from the Roumanian *berbec*, sheep, mutton, hence probably dating from the Crimean War. Tinned meat also passed under the names of *langouste de caillou*, ' pebbly crawfish ', with which compare *légume bien tendre* as French prisoners of war at Göttingen styled herring ; *gorille* ; and especially *singe*. This last dates from about 1895 ; the natives of Bassam ate and still eat smoked monkey, and French troops had to follow suit on one of their campaigns. Excellent though it be as a reserve, such meat, if eaten at all regularly, offends as much by its lack of pleasing character as by its positive dryness ; the scorn applied to monkeys in general has, psychologically, its part in the War connotation as well as in the original denotation of the word *singe*.

Bread, the veritable staff of life in 1914–18, is honoured with numerous nicknames and slang names. *Briffeton*, perhaps related to the Poilu *briffer*, to eat, was much less used than *brigeton*. *Brison* and *briston* are interchangeable. *Kaka* is biscuit-bread or, among prisoners, ordinary bread : often as *pain kaka*, from *k.k. brot*, which, as the German Army loaf, represents *kaiserliches Kriegs-Brot* : the two letters *k.k.* having been read with their alphabetical value. (In Germany such bread is generally called ' kappa ', from the Greek *k* often used as an abbreviation.) *Brot*, rare in the trenches but common in the prison-camps in Germany, was in the latter applied correctly to German bread. *Delikatessen*, which in Germany is applied to sausagery and cold meats, designates bread roasted in oil. *Brutal*, more usual for a cannon (especially in *faire tousser le brutal*) and, chiefly pejorative, for wine. *Croubs, croups, croums*, from the Arabic *khoubz*, made little headway outside of the African regiments. *Croûte* also meant soup, or even food in general, and a meal, the last from the Parisian *croûter*, to eat, whence *croustaille* and *croustance*, likewise a meal. *Grignolet*, excellently treated by Esnault, appears in Barbusse's 'Le Feu' and has the variant *brignolet*: it derives either from *grigne*, usual in Paris since 1718, the crack in a well-baked crust and the golden colour of such a crust, or from *grignon*, a piece of crusty bread or of biscuit; compare *gringue*, also in 'Le Feu'.

Maroc is a Piedmontese word, not *Maroc*, Morocco; *meule*, a mould, and *pierre à affûter*, whetstone, are obvious pejoratives; *pso(u)mi* derives from modern Greek. Munition bread was sometimes known as *Saint-Honoré*; any bread, *boule*.

Fasting had a bevy of synonyms, many being variants of the standard colloquial *se mettre la ceinture*; 'to tighten one's belt', as *se mettre la bride, se mettre la corde*, and *se mettre la tringle*, the third recalling the Parisian workman's *tringle*, nothing, which dates from c. 1890. *Briques* accounts for *bouffer des briques, manger des briques, s'enfiler des briques*, and the facetious *se caler des briques, sauce cailloux*. The basic idea of eating something so hard that one could not possibly eat it is synonymous with 'to eat nothing', hence 'to have nothing to eat', and is present in the further phrases: *becqueter du bois, manger* or *becqueter des clarinettes*; *clopes*, in the following, signifies cigarette-ends: *becqueter* or *s'enfoncer* or *se taper* or *s'envoyer des clopes*. Rather different are *lire le journal* and *jouer du fifre*, both pre-War and local.

More cheerful, or at least not so wry-mouthed, are the synonyms for drink. *Blindé* bears only a false resemblance to the English slang 'blind' from 'blind drunk', for it means armoured, i.e. impenetrably, hence insuperably drunk. *Frigorifié* is of doubtful origin. *Muraille* has been correctly developed from *mûr*, pre-War slang of the same meaning. *Noir*, drunk, has nothing to do with *le noir*, boredom. *Rétamé* is connected with tinkering, *rondard* from *rond* in the sense of frank, easy-going; *plein* corresponds with our 'full'. *Brindezingue* occurs either as *être brindezingue* or *être dans les brindezingues*: Déchelette says that it derives from *brindes*, toasts (presumably by echoic change-repetition); tentatively I suggest that the term may have been influenced by *brin de zinc*, the last word understood in the sense of a bistro, a cheap wine- and coffee-shop. Yet other terms are *barre*; *blet*, literally 'going bad', of fruit; *bout de bois*; *gaz*; (*être* or *avoir son*) *grain*; *en désordre*; *retourné*: *bousillé*; *chocolat*, which, being a synonym also for a coloured soldier, explains why *sénégalais* means drunk; *fait* or *refait*, 'done to a turn'; *réussi*; (especially *bien*) *conditionné*; *mort* and *cuit*, both pre-War; *faisandé* literally 'high', of game; *raide*; *mélangé*, from the usual effect of mixing one's drinks; *zingué* belongs to the family of *blindé* and *rétamé*; with *goudronné*, literally tarred, compare *noir* and *chocolat*; *schlass* (or *chass*), as used by Barbusse, and perhaps from the German *geschlossen*. *Zigzag*, says Esnault, is due to the American soldiers, but he also admits that the words may have been a development from French dialect.

Often a man, no matter what his nationality, got

drunk in order to forget either the horror or the despondent depression caused by trench-warfare. Classic French speaks of *spleen*, taken from the English writers of the first half of the eighteenth century ; colloquial French now says *cafard*, a word firmly established before 1914 by the French Army in Africa and wonderfully popularized by the War ; *coup de cafard* was any foolish or serious or suicidal act caused by such depression. Worse than *le cafard* was *le cafard noir*, worse again the *cafard vert*, this last being equivalent to the more learned *hypercafard*. One could bemoan a man *cafardisé, encafardé*, thus despondent, or congratulate him on being *décafardé, désencafardé*, cured of ' the blue devils '. Synonyms are few but noteworthy : *bourdon*, from a confusion or a fusion of the various senses of that word in ordinary French ; *le noir*, similar to the poetical *papillons noirs* ; *se cailler le raisiné*, to be depressed ; *avoir le typhus*, rather more frequent for the same affliction, which might also be expressed by either *être dans ses grises* or *avoir la grise*, less sombre than *le noir* ; *tranchéite*, spleen caused by the trenches ; *flemme, cosse*, and *veson* were ascending stages of the same complaint ; *le veson rouge* is dangerous, *le veson noir* quite incurable.

One could, however, understand why soldiers imprisoned in Germany fell victims to *le veson noir* or even *le cafard vert*. The language of the French prisoners, as of the English, was even more macaronic than argotic ; it contained words borrowed from fellow-prisoners of other nationalities, but especially it employed many German words, of which Dauzat archly says : ' As a secret language it would have been difficult to find anything more apt to put their jailors off the scent.' He draws attention to one 'secret' cant expression: *vingt-deux*, a conventional warning customary to French criminals as far back as the days of Vidocq and adopted enthusiastically by other nationals to circumvent the German guards. Coffee was called *jus de fèves*, which receives point from the popularity of *jus* as coffee among the unimprisoned Poilus. The German censorship was called *tante Anastasie*, prisons *Dardanelles*, and dungeons ('black holes' is the more correct military term) *sous-marins*. The Prussian flag hoisted to signalize a German victory was always called *le charognard*, from *charogne*, carrion or a blackguard. French prisoners called the particled among them: *chevaux de luxe*, *noms démontables*, *noms à courant d'air*, and *noms à charnière*, the fourth being probably suggested by the third. The Russians were called *Karachos*, from the Russian word for good; from Russian came *niet*, no(t), *sto*, what?, and *eto*, it is. The officers, who had tennis-courts, took from English *ready* and *play*, often corrupted to *radis* and *prêt*; all ranks spoke of a *half-mark*, the unit of cash exchange. The principal German words adopted were these: *gefangen*, a prisoner, *arbeit*, work, *gut*, good, and more often *nicht gut*, bad; *krank*, ill or sick, *brief*, a letter; *commando*, slightly changed to mean a body of prisoners working outside a camp; *cap(o)ut*, dead, killed, or finished, indeed a kind of word of all work; *brot* and *kaka*, noted above; *kartoffel*, a potato; 'meat had no name: one never saw meat'; the German numerals, those ending in *-ig* being pronounced *-ich*; *kolossal*; *planmaessig* (frequent in the German communiques), according to plan, especially of a retreat; *pfennig*

THE SLANG OF THE POILU 179

pronounced either as in German or as *fennich* or even as *péniche* ; *morgenfrüh,* ' to-morrow morning ', i.e. never, the Germans using the phrase as a convenient postponement ; *verboten,* often pronounced *faire beau temps* ; *ersatz-girl,* a temporary sweetheart ; *beschlagnahem,* to confiscate ; *zuruck,* back !, go away ! ; *ça stimmt,* that's all right, that's good, that's agreed ; and a few other words and phrases.

With the German words used by the French prisoners of war we may compare the following, employed by the British soldiers imprisoned in Germany. *Kamerad !* did facetious duty for stop ! I've had enough of that ! *Nix,* nothing, was not unknown before the War. *Strafe,* noun and verb (punish, admonish), extended, like *kamerad,* throughout the British Army ; *counter-strafe,* in the special sense of to take reprisals, belonged to the vocabulary of officers and artillerymen. The frequency of *abort,* a water-closet, in the conversation of, and in books written by, British prisoners of war in Germany is due solely to the fact that there could they best devise and discuss, thence sometimes best execute, their plans for escape. *Ak dum* denoted a German notice-board, which, more likely than not, would be headed *Achtung !* Deviation of sense characterizes *arbeit,* properly work, but usually understood to mean a work-camp for prisoners. *Biskiwits,* variant *biskwitz,* were those maize biscuits which were sometimes obtainable from the prison-camp canteens in Germany. (*C*)(*K*)*aracho*(*u*) good, as among the French, amounted in fact to a prisoner's lingua francal word, a kind of skeleton-key to all conversation. *Dullmajor* was the term applied to the interpreters provided by the Germans. *Ersatz,* as indicated above, denoted any, but especially an inferior, substitute ; *kapout*, dead or finished, was like *nix gut*, another link-word among the prisoners of all nations. *Garnisonlazarett* was adopted, unchanged, for a military hospital. Also direct from German, but by the British spelt without the substantival capital : *kriegsgefangen(er)*, a prisoner of war ; *kriegsgarnisonarrestanstalt*, a military prison ; *kriegsgeleit*, a military escort ; *kriegsgericht*, a court martial ; *Kriegsministerium*, the German War Office. *Hans Wurst*, as at the Front, constituted the German 'opposite member' to Tommy Atkins. *Landsturm* and *Landwehr*, the third and the second reserve of the German Army, were in constant use : so were the reserves. *Schwarz brot* or simply *brot* was, of course, the German black bread. *Spurlos versenkt*, literally sunk without trace, soon came to mean lost untraceably, disappeared, gone, whether of man, beast, or thing ; curiously enough, one of the London morning newspapers, just after the last General Election, had, in reference to the Labour Party, the notice-board headline : *Sunk Without Trace*.

SOLDIERS' SLANG OF THREE NATIONS

WITH the adequate lexicography now available soldiers' slang of 1914-18 has come into its own. France, Germany and England have excellent dictionaries of this characteristic and vital speech.

Omitting various small works,[1] we find that France has three glossaries, Germany one, England two. The French are François Déchelette's ' L'Argot des Poilus ', 1918, a book with 1,100 entries and much wit, good humour, lively writing, alert intellect, and delightfully readable ' essayettes ' on the principal words ; Albert Dauzat's ' L'Argot de la Guerre ', 1918, second edition 1919, a work containing not only a condensed and admirably clear vocabulary of 1,650 entries but a long and very important study on language (general and particular) in its relation to the Great War ; and Gaston Esnault's ' Le Poilu tel qu'il se parle ', 1919, the frankest and the fullest work (1,800 entries), as erudite as Dauzat's but less attractively written than either of the other two volumes. The German glossary appeared in 1925 : ' Schwere Brocken ', compiled by Sigmund Graff (author of ' Meine Fresse ') and

[1] Of these the most notable is the ' Wörterbuch der wichtigsten Geheim-und Berufssprachen ' by Dr. Erich Bischoff, who includes soldiers' and sailors' slang along with cant, Yiddish, theatrical slang, &c. The first edition appeared towards the end of the War ; my edition is the second, undated.

Walter Borman and wittily, realistically illustrated by Edward Thöny, is, of all the dictionaries listed here, the most efficient in manner and the tersest in definition ; it contains nearly 3,000 words, a number of word-groups, and a list of sayings such as will be found in none of the French books and is paralleled only in Brophy's work. In 1925, also, Messrs. Fraser and Gibbons published their valuable ' Soldier and Sailor Words and Phrases ', the first to do justice to the ' slanguage ' of the Tommy ; five years later, John Brophy published his ' Songs and Slang of the British Soldier ', of which the third edition, very greatly enlarged (the glossary entries totalling 2,000), came out in September 1931.

One knows that the French, the Germans and the English lament the fact that no adequate record survives of the slang of the Napoleonic Wars ; even that of the Crimean and the Franco-Prussian Wars is represented only by a few meagre and disconnected scraps. This regret may serve to indicate the true value of what the conventional tend to consider the riff-raff of speech, the purists as an ugly and unimportant corruption, and the more narrow-minded champions of the honour of the Army as perhaps an affront and certainly an uncomfortable misrepresentation. The truth is that behind a war vocabulary there lies a significant and complex psychology, to which justice can be done neither by lengthy active service undirected by essential scholarliness nor by the most imposing erudition unsweetened and ' unpragmatized ' by at least two years' service in the field [1] ; neither of these

[1] It is doubtless my prejudice as a mere private, but I believe that an educated private or ' non-com.' can deal better with

incomplete equipments can hope to set forth, responsibly and equitably, the true meaning of soldiers' slang.

Of each of the French, German and English military slangs it is possible to say that while the foreign contributions are significant they are, in the last analysis, very much more picturesque and interesting than basically important. The mixing of the classes has been far more influential than the mixing of the nations. This mixing has, moreover, been more profitable to the educated than to the uneducated : for the latter picked up little more than some arresting or grandiloquent journalese and some useful officialese ; the former gained immensely by their acquisition of vivid popular words and phrases and by their perception of the vitality and immediacy characteristic no less of dialect than of urban slang—indeed, many cultured men that had been in danger of becoming effete, pretty-pretty, or wire-drawn, were revivified by contact with their less 'respectable' fellows.

The city has exercised a greater influence than the country. Low urban slang—Parisian *argot*, Berlin *Slang*, and *Cockney*—appealed not only to the countryman but to the highbrow and the near-highbrow. In peace-time, the cultured hold the ascendancy ; in war-time, the populace gains the upper-hand. Such a 'reaction' is beneficial to any language, for despite the vulgarisms and the solecisms that become general,

soldiers' slang than an officer can. Otherwise I should deplore the fact that there are, in England alone, three Professors of English who, with very fine War records, have done nothing towards that critical dictionary of our soldiers' slang which I desiderate ; one of them, however, provided me with some valuable notes for the third edition of 'Songs and Slang'.

it prevents that fixing of the vocabulary which both aristocracy and bureaucracy try to enforce ; nor is the effect of war's dynamic ' maltreatment ' of a language confined to the armies engaged.

It is unsafe to generalize on the differences of the slang employed by Poilu, Gerry and Tommy, but one can at least say that the first was the most witty, mocking and realistic, the second the most technical, blasphemous and grim, the third the most direct, the most obvious and the best humoured. In all three, the influence of the Regular Army was somewhat less powerful than that of civilian Paris, Berlin, London ; thieves' slang, like rhyming and back slang, was much less operative in German than in the two others ; all three were, in fact, less cynical and Rabelaisian than they appeared to be ; all three frequently harked back to home-life in their figures of speech ; all three stressed food, drink, civilian comforts ; all three tended to materialize the spiritual and to brutalize the material, though the exceptions are many ; and all three were sly or depreciatory in their references to their military superiors, as they were to politicians and other noisy stay-at-homes, French being the most biting, German the most pessimistic, and English the most tolerantly contemptuous. Comradeship, solidarity, patient courage, and the tendency either to ironize or to belittle one's fears, sufferings and discomforts : these qualities were common to, and equally characteristic of, the soldiers of France, Germany, England. Moreover, these soldier-slangs contain no slanderous nor insulting names for the combatant foe ; such amenities being reserved for politicians, profiteers, pressmen, and for the subtler barbarism of peace.

The comparison of particular groups of synonyms will, however, yield more concrete results, most of which speak sufficiently loudly for themselves to render interpretation and deduction supererogatory. To avoid the charge of cooking the facts, I do not choose at all, but give all the synonyms recorded in the various above-mentioned glossaries.

The rifle attracts few English, but many French and German synonyms. The commonest French term is *flingue* (with *flingot* as frequent variant), perversely from the German *flinte* ; *Oscar* and *seringue* (syringe) are popular ; other synonyms are *petoir, raide, tue-boches, soufflet* (bellows), *nougat, clarinette, lance-pierres* (stone-thrower, sling) and *arbalète* (cross-bow). With the last compare the German *Flitzbogen*, of the same denotation. Perhaps the two most used German synonyms are *Gewehr* and *Braut* (the soldier's bride), the latter dating from at least as early as 1900 as soldiers' slang, as do *Kuhfuss* (crow-bar), *Knarre* (rattle), and *Schiessprügel* (Brown Bess) ; common are *Karline* and *Laura* ; other terms were *Schiesseisen* (shooting iron) and *Kracheisen* (din-iron, crack-weapon), *Kusine* and *Tante*, both from the French ; *Latte*, a lath ; *Spritze*, same as the French *seringue* ; and *Schinken*, ham, probably short for *Schinkenbein*, a ham-bone. The English terms current in 1914–18 are *bundook*, from the Arabic for a fire-arm, originally a cross-bow, though the soldier undoubtedly took the word from Hindustani ; of Regular Army heredity, as is the phrase *bundook and spike*, rifle and bayonet. So too is *hipe*, perhaps a corruption of *pike* ; probably, however, it is an N.C.O.'s makeshift-noise, so much more easy than *arms* in, e.g., *slope arms*. *Gruel-stick* is less common.

Some Tommies, the more learned, call the French rifle *Lebel Ma'm'selle* or *Ma'm'selle Lebel*, from the name of the inventor, M. Lebel; these two terms, coming from the Poilu, represent a form of rhyming slang punning on *la belle*.

The bayonet likewise has many names. The Poilu calls it *cure-dents*, which is the exact equivalent of Tommy's *tooth-pick* and Gerry's *Zahnstocher*; *aiguille*, needle, and *aiguille à tricoter* (knitting-needle), *fourchette*, a very popular term to which the German *Kröstenstecher*, and the English *toasting-fork* correspond closely enough; *fourchette à escargots*, snail-fork, is probably the original of the preceding term; with *tire-bouchon*, cork-screw (punned as *tire-Boches*), compare *Büchsenöffner*, the equivalent of Tommy's *tin-opener*; analogous to *coupe-choux*, cabbage-knife, are *Käsemesser*, cheese-measure or jack-knife, *Kräppelspiess*, grapesticker, *Krautmesser*, a Bavarian word meaning krautmeter, *Schnitzer*, carving-knife, *Spargelstecher*, asparagusknife, and *Distelstecher*, thistle-sticker, and the English *meat-skewer*; the German *Splint*, linch-pin, has no fellow, though the second member appears in the English *winkle-pin* and the Poilu speaks of *épingle*, pin; French offers nothing to balance *Baugenett* and *bagonet*, the latter (undoubtedly prompting the former) being a very common early form of the modern *bayonet* and taken over from the Regular Army; on the other hand the French *tournebroche*, turn-spit, has a solus position; compare, however, the related and punning *enfile-boche*, Boche-threader or -beader, and *rince-Boche*, approximately rinse-Boche; the French have no companion for *Ratzenstecher*, polecat-sticker, or for *catstabber*; Tommy's humorous *persuader* stands alone, as do the following Poilu terms : *tachette*, dialectal for a small round-headed nail, and *clou*, plain nail ; [*la chose*] *luisante*, the shiner ; *Joséphine*, heard occasionally, and *Rosalie*, heard very often indeed, though many Poilus avoided it because of its literary origin, it being due to Theodore Botrel, who launched it in the 'Bulletin des Armées' on 4 November 1914, as a kind of pendant to the ancient *Durandal*. Still more used among the Poilus themselves is *fourchette* : but, as Déchelette tells us quite definitely, *ils emploient généralment le mot français ' baïonette '*, just as the British troops usually say *bayonet* and the German soldiers *Bajonett* or *Seitengewehr*.

The *Stahlhelm*, *casque de tranchée* (slangily *casque en fer*), *steel-helmet* attracts attention. *Bache* is Parisian argot and without an exact equivalent. The hat connotation appears in *bourgignotte*, *cloche*, *melon*, *toque* and *chapeau* itself (whence *blindé*, armoured hat), as in *steel-jug* and *tin-hat* (the latter much the commoner) and as in *Feld-*, *Gefechts-* and *Gelände-hut*, field-, battle-, country hat—in *Römerdeckel*, Roman cap—in *Gefechtshaube*, battle-cap, like the English *battle-bowler*—in *Offensivhut*—and in *Sturm-hut* and *-zylinder*, storm-hat and -screen ; with the last of these German compounds one naturally aligns *Kriegszylinder*, war-cylinder, *Angströhre*, fear-cylinder, and the rather beautiful *Gewittertulpe*, the tulip of the storm. Of the mainly culinary type are *lid* and *pudden-basin*, the former being equally popular with *tin-hat* and the second corresponding roughly with the German *Waschbecken*, wash-basin ; *Brockenfänger*, dust-bin ; *Kochkessel*, caldron, goes with *marmite* and *casserole* ; *bocal* (a wide-necked bottle), *bol*, *soupière*, *saladier*, *panier à salade* ; *éteignoir*, an extinguisher, very aptly from its shape. *Boutrole* is somewhat more recondite, for it is suggested by the form and the shape of a *bouterolle*, the iron tip of a scabbard. The shape likewise determines *pot de fleurs* and *pot de chambre*, the latter matching with Gerry's *Nachtpott*; shape slightly, humorous analogy greatly, prompts *Schrapnellschirn*, shrapnel-screen, with its variant *-zylinder*, shrapnel-case. *Wetterverteiler*, weather-divider, has no parallel, while *Stellungsgoks* is dialectal and obscure. Finally the French take *Blockhaus*, pill-box, to describe the steel-helmet.

Haversack has fewer synonyms; this comparative paucity is due in part to the fact that some of its slang designations are loosely interchangeable with those of the knapsack. There are only two German terms: *Hungersack*, *Klammersack* (holdfast-bag). And only two English: *jolah*, a Regulars' word from India; *scranbag*, also pre-War, *scran* dating back to *c.* 1870 in its two senses of food in general, a meal in particular. The Poilus, however, have some ten words: *armoire* and *armoire à glace*, the latter being a fantastic development; *as* and *as de carreau*, ace of diamonds, in allusion to its shape; *valise*, a playful use of a typically civilian word, with perhaps a wistful regret; *compteur à gaz*, gas-meter, very rarely heard after 1915; *fainéant*, idler, for it is to be carried; *Philibert* and *Azor*, the latter a deliberate corruption of *as* similar to that of *gau* (a louse) into *la famille Gautier*; *vésicatoire*, 'métaphore de sensation musculaire' (Esnault); *dur*, primarily from its hardness against one's left side, with a further allusion to the 'iron rations' therein carried.

But the haversack is only one of the many objects

carried by the P.B.I., a term rarely used by 'the poor b——y infantry' themselves. The foot-soldier, the *fantassin*, the *Infanterist*, coins—or is given—some picturesque and significant names. The English names are *Camel Corps*, collective; *grabby*, from the Crimean War; *tray*, generally in the plural, probably from the normal use of that useful household article, *something to hang things on* being indeed a synonym; *beetle-crusher*, meaning also an Army boot; *mud-crusher*, dating from about 1880, is of the same group as the German *Dreckfresser*, mud-eater, 'mud-lark', *Dreckstampfer*, mud-stamper, *Schlammtreter*, mud-treader, and *Lkaenputscher*, puddle-splasher, as well as the merely referable *Grabenscheisser* or the French *écrase-merde*; and especially *foot-slogger*, the most used of all. *Footslogger* is the late nineteenth- and early twentieth-century counterpart of the eighteenth-century *foot-wobbler*; similar are the French *marche-à-pieds* and *pousse-caillou*, pebble-pusher, and the German *Fusslatscher*, foot-shuffler, and analogous are *Kilometer-fresser* and *-schwein*, kilometre-eater and -pig or glutton. The 'animal world' furnishes several interesting terms, for the French have *chat*, the artillery's designation of the less fortunate arm of the service, *écrevisse de rampart*, trench-crawfish, *bigorneau*, periwinkle, and *mille-pattes*, a centipede, this last a delightfully apt 'father to the thought'; the Germans *Blindschleiche*, a slowworm, *Feldmaüse*, fieldmouse, *Sand-hase* (and *-latscher*), sand-hare (and -sloven). Rural also is *Stoppelhopfer*, stubble-hopper. *Kanonenfutter*, cannon-fodder, dates from long before the War; never very popular with British troops, who, for the most part, found the joke rather too grim. Proper names are restricted to the German *Hannes*,

Hans, Johnnie, and *Hansl*, the Bavarian form of the same; the punning *Has! Has!* is the artillery's slightly jeering name for 'poor old Gerry' and reminds us that *troufion* prompts the usually urbane, even if trenchantly witty Déchelette to write: ' It is thus that the infantryman is baptized disdainfully by the cavalry and artillery, who, as everyone knows, are of a superior essence . . . There is always one half of the world mocking the other, even at the front.' Slightly martial are *lignard*, the man of the front line, and *griveton*, *grifeton*, *grifton*, from the *grive* that, in Parisian argot, means a guard or war. *Bibi* means either an ordinary soldier or an infantryman and it represents a diminutive of *biffin*, very common in this sense, *les gars de la biffe* being also the infantry; *biffin* is an obvious abbreviation. The word *fantassin* leads to some quaint transformations, of which the best known is *fantaboche*, *fantabosse*, by way of the execrable pun, *fente à sein*, whence *fente à bosse*, whence . . . ; *fantoche* abbreviates *fantaboche*, which by manipulation gives also *bobosse* (not much used by the infantryman himself), *chabosse* (rare), and *dachebosse*, a fusion of *fantabosse* with *Dache*. German dialect is responsible for the obscure *Schniggl* of the Bavarians and the *Piefke* of the North Germans, *Trichterprolet*, mine-, or trench-fellow, chap, the *prolet* being short for *proletariat*. *Musko, muschko, muschkote*, has three senses, each leading naturally from the other, thus: 'infantryman' from 'musketeer', 'the common soldier' from 'infantryman'. *Fussfanterie* puns obviously on *Fuss*, foot, and *[In]fanterie*, and is translatable as foot-puppery. *Backzahn* is subtle, for, meaning back-tooth, it infers that as such a tooth, though not much seen, is exceedingly useful, so the infantryman, though little in the limelight, yet does most of the work.

His home was a *dug-out, abri, Unterstand*. Here the words fall into no easy groups, and are seen best in three national lists. The German terms are *Grotte, U-Boot* (U Boat), *Raucherabteil* (smoking-compartment), *Bollen-keller* and *-lock* (onion-cellar, -hole), *Bau* and *Fuchsbau* (kennel, fox's), *Helden-keller* and *-röhre* (heroes' cellar, shaft) ; a reinforced concrete dug-out is called *Bunker*, a very large dug-out a *Tonhalle*, a concert-hall, while a makeshift shelter is *Kaninchenloch*, a rabbit-warren, a very small one a *Zigarrenkiste*, a cigar-box, a very wet one *Kaltwasserheilanstalt*, a sanatorium ; other names were *Laden*, meeting-place, *Tapferkeits-stollen*, valour-gallery, and *Villa Blindgänger* or *Bückdich*, or *Feldgrau*, &c., the Villa Blindgoer or Stooping or Field-Grey, &c. The English slang synonyms are few : the small dug-outs are *cubby-holes*, those so small as to be mere ostrich-pretences are *funk-holes*, while the smallish are *glory-holes* ; *dosh* was the generic Canadian name. The French synonymy is both more considerable and more interesting than either the German or the English. The following are of native origin : *canfouine*, little used ; *carrée*, occasionally ; *cagibi*, from *cage* and *bi*, a common argotic suffix ; *case*, among soldiers on the Eastern front—a lingua franca word ; *métro*, 'the underground', one large enough for an infantry section and having two exits ; *calebasse*, already employed analogously by Barbey d'Aurevilly ; *camigeotte*, found, like the preceding, in Barbusse's ' Le Feu ' ; *guignol*, only big enough for one person ; *pé-cé*, from *Poste de Commandement*. The genuinely foreign words (not words that, like *case* and *calebasse*, are merely of foreign derivation) are these : *estanco*, from the Spanish for a tobacco-shop ; *tata*, which, in use only on the various staffs, is of obscure origin ; *kasba*, an Eastern word used only on that front ; popular are the Arabic words *gourbi* and *guitoune*, extremely popular the Annamite *cagna(t)*—the first, the oldest in army use, meaning literally an earth-built house, the second meaning a (camp-) tent, the third deriving from cai-nha, a bamboo house, as in Léra's ' Tonkinoiseries ', 1896.

For the next three groups—*thingummy, no man's land (streitiges Gebiet), barbed wire (stechelzaundraht)*, there are no generally used German slang terms ; with this compare the fact that while the Germans and French have numerous words for a machine-gun, the Tommy has none. For *thingummy*, Tommy says *oojah*, with variants *oojah-ka-piv, oojah-cum-pivvy*, and *oojiboo*, the Canadian *hooza-ma-kloo* ; and the Poilu *truc*, with the ' rhyming ' development *trucmuche*, while the Zouaves favoured *chuchemahure*, of Algerian origin ; *truc* has long been the general civilian word.

No man's land, besides having no synonym in German slang, has none in English ; and only three in French. *Bled* is fairly common : originally it meant the Moroccan *brousse* or ' bush '—wild and uncultivated country. *Tapis* was heard at times. More popular, however, was *billard*, billiard-table. Barbed wire likewise possesses slang synonyms in neither German nor English, while in French it is called *barbelé* from *fil de fer barbelé* and, by way of a pun, *barbouillé*. Thence to *over the top with the best of luck* (after 1916 the *luck* was tacitly omitted) it is a short step. The English phrases for a charge or an attack are *over the top, over the lid* (in 1916 only), *over the plonk*, and, as verbs also, *hop over* and *go over*. Here, German is less rich ; *gib ihm !*, like *drauf !*, is the command. French easily the richest. *A la barbaque !* is ' charge ! '—with the bayonet ; *barbaque* is an old Parisian slang word for meat, but it comes from the Crimea ; *sauter le barriau*, to climb the parapet (in order to attack, to trot across no man's land) ; *se bigorner*, with the pejorative variants *se faire bigorner, aller* or *monter à la bigorne* ; *monter sur le billard*, which also means to mount the operating table ; *monter sur le tapis* ; *monter sur le plateau* ; *foncer dans le bled, dans la brousse,* and *dans le brouillard*, where *foncer* has the sense ' to charge with the head down ', like a goat ; *aller à la châtaigne* ; *monter aux petites echelles*, to climb the short ladders sometimes provided for clambering into no man's land from a difficult trench ; *fantaisie sur fil de fer*, usually a nightmare and not a fantasy ; *à la fourchette !* of an attack with bayonets fixed ; *lâchons tout* also means *allons à l'attaque !* ; *aux pluches*, not so common for *à la charge !* ; *aller au séchoir*, to attack positions that have their barbed wire intact and well defended, where the implicit idea is that which is expressed more explicitly in *sécher sur le fil*, ' hanging on the old barbed wire ' ; *monter à la ripée*, to leave the comforting trench for the naked parapet, a phrase that one philologist considers to have at first been *monter à l'R.I.P.*, which is just a little too clever to be probable ; *sauter le toboggan* ; and *valse lente !* as an order, though one very rarely—except for a distance of 300 yards or less— went at anything more rapid than a slow jog-trot : carrying the weight one did, one could not run—except to dodge a burst (if, indeed, one heard or saw it at all).

In the hop-over, many hoped for and some got a wound sufficiently serious to cause them to be sent ' home ' without being a prospective burden to themselves. The terms for ' wounded ' are for the most part realistic, either humorously or resignedly or grimly. The right sort of wound receives commendation in *sénateur*, a man seriously wounded or ill—as opposed to a *député* ; in *Heimat-schuss* or *-trellerchen*, a ' home '-shot (wound) or *-puller*, and in *deutschlandverdachtig*, suspicious, or smacking, of Germany ; and in *have* or *get* or *cop a Blighty* or *a Blighty one*. The phrase *to cop a packet* may mean to be fatally wounded, but often it signifies the lesser wounding ; French offers no parallel. German has the phrases *kriegen* (to catch it), *eins vor den Ballon kriegen, einen an dem Latz* [pinafore] *kriegen, einen an dem Pinsel* [head] *kriegen, ein Stuck Eisen ins Kreuz kriegen* (to be severely wounded), *einen gebrannt* or *draufgebrannt kriegen* (to catch it hot), to which add the analogous phrases *ein Ding (verpasst) bekommen*, to get something (forgotten or lost), and *verpassen*, to miss something. Other German synonyms are *abfrühstücken*, to breakfast away (sometimes, to be killed) ; *angekratzt*, scratched, cf. *kitzeln*, to tickle ; *angetötet werden*, to be gravely wounded ; *eine Motte gewischt kriegen*, to rub against a moth. The French terms not yet mentioned are *amoché*, which in Parisian pre-War slang meant either spoilt or hurt in an accident ; *attigé*, touched, ultimately from the Latin *attingere* ; *avoir un accroc*, to get one's clothes torn ; *conditionné* ; *bien servi*, well served ; *complet* ; *fadé*, lucky ; *avoir son compte*, to get one's dues ; *se faire courber une aile*, to get a wing ' bent ' ; *sucré*, sweetened ; *assaisonné*, seasoned ; *salé*, salted. The remaining Tommy synonyms are *pipped*, especially by a bullet whether of rifle, revolver, or machine-gun ; *to stop one*, to be wounded by bullet or shell-fragment ; *tap*, a wound, as in ' a nice little tap on the shoulder '. It may be noted that the wounded were either *walking wounded* or *stretcher cases*.

To perish in battle or in the fighting zone, either killed immediately or dying soon of the wound, has still more synonyms, as might be expected from the finality of such a fate. The German expressions are *glauben*, to have faith, to be a believer ; *kalten Arm kriegen*, to catch a cold arm ; *parti gehen*, to go to a party ; *der alte Herr Heldentod*, old Mr. Heroes'-Death ; *es hat ihm das G'stell z'ammdraht*, brought to the stretcher ; *über den Harz gehen*, to cross the Rubicon ; *um die Ecke gehen* (a pre-War colloquialism), to go round the corner ; another pre-War colloquialism, *ins Gras biessen*, to bite the dust, is seen, in its literal form (to bite the grass), to bear some resemblance to *dépoter son géranium*, to unpot one's flowers, to die, and *avoir un petit jardin sur le ventre*, to have a garden on one's belly, to be dead and buried, and especially *manger les pissenlits par la racine* or *manger les salades par le trognon* ; the two *manger* phrases afford excellent parallels to *push up daisies*, (later) *be daisy-pushing*, which glorious expressions may have been influenced by the much feebler pre-War civilian slang, *to turn up one's toes to the daisies*, found first in Barham's ' Ingoldsby Legends ', 1837 ; *a daisy-pusher*, by the way, is a fatal wound, and *to become a landowner* means to be dead and buried, the grave being the estate. The other French terms for ' to be killed ' are these : *se laisser tomber*, to let oneself fall ; *se faire bigorner*, with which contrast the already cited *se bigorner* ; *être brûlé*, to be burnt (against which set *einen gebrannt kriegen* of the preceding paragraph), *brûler*, as ' to kill ', dating from Stendhal, 1836 ; *être gaspillé*, to be wasted, meaning also to be wounded ; *se faire niquer*, the latter verb coming from lingua franca ; *en jouer* or *être évacué sur une toile de tente*, to play a role in a sheet of canvas ; *avoir la grande permission*, to go on long furlough ; *sécher sur le fil*, to be dead but not buried ; *être dézingué*, to have one's zinc removed ; *être dégringolé*, more usually in the active voice ; *se faire paumer*, from *paumer*, to lay hands upon ; *être bousillé, ébousillé*, especially of disruptive death by shell-burst ; *être but*, connected with *but*, end ; *être capout*, from the German ; *avoir* or *gagner la croix de bois*, which, meaning to earn a wooden cross, recalls Dorgelès' ' Les Croix de Bois ', perhaps the finest of all War novels ; *être décollé*, to be decapitated ; *être descendu*, but chiefly in the active voice, as in *to lay low* ; *disparaître*, to disappear ; *claboter, clapoter*, and *clamecer, clamser*, and *clasper* (virtually the same word as *clamser*), all of death swift-coming from wounds ; *claquer*, whether on or off the field—a very old civilian slang word ; *être escofié*, like *être bousillé* or *zigouillé* (echoic, this), refers to death on the battle-field ; *être estourbi*, generally in the active, is from the German ; *être étalé*, to be laid out for show ; *être évacué* ; *être fauché*, to be mown down ; *être suriné*, pre-War Parisian ; and *virer le ventre pour voir passer les aéros*, to turn one's belly about to see the aeroplanes pass ; the English synonyms for death, the process of death, and the state of death, are less numerous than the French, more numerous than the German. *Wiped out*, whether of one's person or one's military unit ;

loaf o' bread, by rhyming slang for dead ; *mafeesh*, from Arabic, and rarely heard, except among Regulars and Anzacs, on the Western front ; *napoo*, meaning also finished, empty, ruined, from *il n'y en a plus* ; *off it*, to die (never adjectivally) ; *snuff it* (pre-War), *to be buzzed*, from *to buzz*, to send a message on the *buzzer*, the portable telephone officially known as *D mark 3* or *D 3* ; *finee*, Tommyese for *fini* ; *scuppered*, originally nautical ; *gone trumpet-cleaning*, a pre-War Regular-Army phrase ; *to go home, go out* ; *huffed* ; *out of mess*, dead, *to be put out of mess* (cf. the Naval *lose the number of one's mess*), to be killed ; *to have one's number up*, to be dead, sometimes merely to be in trouble, while *his number is up* signifies either ' he's sure to die ' or, less often, ' he's sure to be found out ' ; *outed*, from boxing ; *to go west*, the finest, most beautiful of all these synonyms, is based on the idea of the setting sun and occurs in Classical Greek.

Perhaps death was preferable to the horrors of a fierce bombardment. There are surprisingly few international terms : to the French synonyms I find no exact equivalents in either German or English ; but German *es pumpert*, it bumps, balances the jocular —*What ho! she bumps!* and *be bumped*, be shelled, while *beplastern* is precisely Tommy's *to plaster*, to shell, especially to shell heavily. The other German synonyms are *beasen*, to befoul ; *einheizen, eingheizt bekommen*, to warm, to be warmed ; *Kartusch, Kaschimbo bekommen*, to come under fire, to catch ' cashimbo ', i.e. to catch ' hell ' ; *Kattun kriegen*, to catch calico, from the noise of torn calico or perhaps from the ensuing need for bandages. The French synonyms are more numerous than either the German, the smallest group, or the English. *Arroser*, to spray ; *ça barde*, they're going it hard !, from a verb signifying to become intense and admirably treated by Esnault ; *busoter*, to bombard, from the Poilu *busot*, a shell ; *il y a de la casse*, the shelling is disastrous ; *ça charribote*, there *are* some shells ! ; *on tire le cordon*, they're pulling the string ; of heavy fighting, including bombardment, *coup de chien, de tabac, de Trafalgar*, and *coup dur* ; *être crapouillé*, to be 'toaded' ; *décoction*, a 'rain' of shells ; *jactance teutonne*, Teutonic bragging, i.e. German shelling ; *faire un jus*, to shell ; *marmiter* (transitively), to bombard with heavy shells ; *qu'est-ce qu'on prend!* we, they are catching it ; *être repéré*, to be shelled after the enemy finds the range ; punning this, *être opéré* ; *se faire souinger* (from boxing), to be ' swinged ', to be shelled, to cause oneself to be shelled ; *faire du tabac*, to bombard ; *zinguer* and *zinziner*, the same, only transitively ; *qu'est-ce qu'on déguste*, we're tasting something ! ; *ça se donne*, to bombard, or to be bombarded, very heavily ; *sonner*, to ring (transitively), from an Apache word meaning to knock against ; *ça tape, there's* a tapping ! ; *ça buque*, same meaning, but from dialect. The English words are : *to bonk*, generally in the passive, and *to plonk*, always in the active, both being echoic ; *crump*, to shell with ' heavies ' ; *blow to b——y*, to shell intensely and intensively ; *cane*, to shell, especially to shell heavily ; *clod*, to shell, nearly always in the active voice ; *strafe*, noun and verb, of a bombardment, cf. *counterstrafe* ; *hate*, a bombardment, from Lissauer's ' Hymn of Hate ', composed in August 1914 ; *pill*, to shell or to bomb ; *iron rations*, shells, shelling ; *iron foundries*, heavy shelling ; *go it*, to bombard, to make an artillery ' demonstration '.

In a bombardment, one looks to one's company, or perhaps one's battalion, Commander, to do the right thing by his men. Yet the nicknames for Captain, Major, Lieutenant-Colonel, and Colonel are comparatively few. The Captain is *the skipper* among officers, *the cap* among the men ; *le vieux, der Alte*, the old man —*Kapitän*, literally a ship's Captain—*Kompanieverfährer*. The Major is *the company's Don Juan, the mage, the maje* ; if the context fits beyond any doubt, *le vieux, der Alte*—*Gottöberst*, God Almighty, on account of his inaccessibility—*Raupenzüchter*, maggot-breeder, a pun on *Raupen*, both maggots and the thick epaulette-fringes distinguishing the higher officers. The Lieutenant-Colonel is *the old man, le vieux*, and in German the same as for a Major. The Colonel is *the old man*, the *kernel* ; *le vieux* ; in German, as for a Major, also *Gottöberster*, God-superior, God-colonel. The Captain, by the way, is also one of *Die 4 Menzel, the four knaves*, i.e. the four Company-Commanders, and, in this capacity, he has a horse, which is known as *Gefechsesel*, battle-donkey. In the British Army, all officers, especially if Colonels or higher, are called generically *the heads*.

In no matter what rank, there are *column-dodgers*, men who evade duty or danger. The German terms are these : *abhauen*, to hide oneself away, to cut oneself off ; *verduften*, to slip away ; *verdünnisieren*, to make oneself scarce, cf. *dünn machen*, to make or play thin, small, scarce ; trench-poets speak feelingly of *verblühen*, decay ; *Aalemann machen*, to play the eel-man, to be slippery ; *Flankenheinrich*, to build a ' flank(ing) Henry ', to show oneself a ' shrewdy '. The French have *tirer une carotte* and *carotter*, pull a carrot, applied chiefly to a 'wangle' effected by plausible speech; *tirer au flanc, au cul*; with the nouns *carotteur, tire(ur) -au-flanc, -au-cul*; and *filocher*, to evade duty or to 'wangle' a good job, the man being a *filocheur*. The English terms are *to dodge the column*; *to swing the lead* (often as *swing it*), of nautical origin, the performer being a *lead-swinger*; cf. *swing the hammer*; a *skrimshanker*, an old Army word; *mike*, to dodge duty or, if it were undodged, to work half-heartedly; *come the old man* or *the old soldier*, to shirk, also to bluff, to domineer; *nut-worker*, i.e. *head-worker*, one who lies awake thinking how to avoid fatigues or the front line.

More attractive is the group of words dealing with rumours (some of which were fantastic in the extreme).[1] German synonyms are of five kinds; the first is based on 'order' or 'instruction', as *Frontbefehl*, an order emanating from the front line, and *Kantinenbefehl*, one heard at a (presumably wet) canteen; that consisting of *Parole*, password or parole; the third, *Kolonnenmärchen, the transport tale* of the British Army but without parallel in the French; the fourth, *Kombüsenbesteck*, a cook's-galley reckoning, estimate, hence story, originally a nautical phrase, to which the French offer the parallel *rapport des cuistots*, a cook's report, and the English *cook-house official*, which last puns on the pejorative use of *British official*, meaning (from mid-1915 till the autumn of 1918) untrustworthy news; and lastly *Latrinen-befehl, -gerucht,* and *-parole*, latrine-order, -rumour, -password—and, late in the War, just (*eine*) *Latrine*—the English term being latrine-rumour, the latrine member being sometimes expressed in vul-

[1] See Stephen Southwold's invaluable essay in 'A Martial Medley', 1931.

garism. The French generally use the word *tuyau*, a pipe, but they also have *mamelouk*, a circularizer of rumours ; *perco*, from *percolateur* ; cf. *jus*, coffee, which is made with a percolator ; *bac*, literally a ferry, probably because ferries are notorious places of exchange for gossip and *canards* ; *bobard*, perhaps from a confusion—or a fusion—of *boniment*, tall stories, patter, with *bobèche*, head ; and *courant d'air*, a draught (of air), because equally intangible. Other English terms are *gup* ; *Furphy*, an Australianism ; *clack* ; and *propaganda*, an officers' word.

Some of these airy nothings are due to fear, which seems to be a very discriminating emotion, for there is only one locution common to even two of the three nations concerned : *les avoir*, to have them (where *les* is *foies* or any other of the synonyms for fear), corresponding to *get 'em*, to get ' the scares '. The French terms are *avoir les chochotes, les colombines*, which, like *avoir mis son pantalon de tremble, chier dans son froc*, and *avoir la chaisse*, mean to have one's bowels unpleasantly perturbed, cf. *avoir la colique, la trouille*, the colic ; *avoir les flubards, avoir* or *mettre les flubes*, pre-War and of uncertain origin ; *avoir les foies, les foies blancs, les foies verts*, even *les foies tricolorés*, to have a liver, to have a liver coloured in one of these picturesque ways ; *avoir les grelots*, to have the shivers ; *avoir* or *mettre les grôles* (or *grolles*) ; *avoir les grelons* is literally synonymous, *grolles* and *grelons* being dialectal for boots ; *avoir les baguettes*, a development from *mettre les baguettes*, to run away, *baguettes* being populace-argot for legs ; *avoir les copeaux*, to have ' the spits ' ; *avoir les jetons*, rare ; *avoir les tricotins*, to have a strong desire to knit with one's legs, i.e. to feel like running away ; *flancher*, to flinch. The Germanisms are less numerous and less vivid ; *Bammel haben*, to be in a funk, a phrase dating from long before the War, as does *Manchetten haben*, from the French *manchettes*, stiff white cuffs, while *Heidenbammel haben* is merely a modern variation on *Heidenangst haben*, literally to have a heathen fear, i.e. to have an unholy fear, to be in a dreadful funk ; *Bollen haben*, to have onions ; *der Arm geht mit Grundeis*, one freezes with fear ; and *Zappen haben*, to have the fidgets. The English words may be few, but they are not insipid : *batchy*, which, in addition to denoting unnerved, also means silly or even mad ; *poggle(d)*, *puggled*, ' rattled ' as well as eccentric and mad-drunk, is a pre-War Regular-Army word ; *off one's rocket*, ' rattled ', also mad ; but, above all, both *have the wind up*, to be afraid, later *have the wind vertical* (neither implying disgrace), and *be windy*, a development from *wind-up*, and definitely pejorative, are genuinely and essentially War words, probably originating in the Air Force.

Fear caused many soldiers to act in a way that brought them to confinement to barracks (*C.B.*) or even to prison. Gerry employs the following terms, some which show a nice sense of humour : *brummen*, to be in prison, a pre-War colloquialism that literally means to grumble ; *dienstfrei sein*, to be service-free, to be off duty, cf. *Freiquartier*, free board and lodging ; *Herberge zur Heimat*, domestic shelter, a roof over one's head ; *Vater Philipp*, Father Philip, and *Vadder Seeman*, daddy sailorman, with which we may compare our own *Paddy Doyle* ; these two words based on furlough (*Urlaub*, itself occasionally used for either arrest or cells) : *Erholungsurlaub*, convalescence-furlough, sick leave ; *Mittelurlaub,* on good behaviour, restricted freedom ; *Kahn,* a boat, which recalls the old English naval term, *stone-frigate* ; *Kasten,* box, paralleled by the French *boîte,* box or tin, *caisse,* case, and *grosse* [*caisse* or *boîte*] as in *il a quatre de grosse, il va à la grosse* (quoted by Déchelette) ; and *Kittchen,* a concrete place, which reminds us both of *jug,* from the eighteenth-century term *stone jug,* and of its derivatives *juggo, jugged,* arrested or imprisoned. The remaining Poilu synonyms are *estanco,* already cited in the sense of dug-out ; *Dardanelles,* a term that, meaning prison, is used among prisoners of war in Germany, where *sous-marin,* a submarine, denotes solitary confinement in a cell ; *hostau, houstau, ousto,* prison, from the word for hostel ; *houste* is a variation on the same root, *ours* a deliberate corruption thereof ; and perhaps the most general, *tôle* (*taule*), an old military term preserved in barracks, the man so punished being *un tôlier, tôlard,* the word meaning literally sheet-iron. The English terms constitute the biggest group, which comprises—in addition to those already mentioned—the following : *clink,* from the ancient criminals' name for a prison in Southwark (London) and echoic of the clinking of fetters, just as *jankers* is of their jangling, the latter term having the specifically military derivatives *jankers men,* defaulters, and *the jankers king,* a provost sergeant ; *cold-storage,* of English origin, and *cooler,* from American thieves' slang ; *bocb* is likewise an American import ; *opera-house* and *glass-house,* the latter a pre-War Regular-Army term, and both employed of detention (-barracks), guard-room, cells, prison ; *spud-hole,* a detention-cell ; *chokey,* from Hindustani, for either guard-room or prison ; *Bow Street,* the orderly-room in relation to company and battalion trials—from the famous old London police-court, the term being unknown among Colonial troops; *hutch*; and *mush*, sometimes spelt and pronounced *moosh*, which, like the preceding word, denotes guard-room or cell(s).

Even in prison, or at the least, in detention, some soldiers managed to ' pinch ' things. This, our last group, contains very few War neologisms and many survivals from old cant. There are, once we account for *réquisitionner*, to *commandeer*, and *acheter*, no exact equivalents in the slang of any one country as compared with the other two, although we notice certain common features, such as euphemism, irony, and a most apt military allusiveness. The Germans have three delicious phrases : *besorgen* (their favourite word), to take care of, *aus Versehen fassen*, to seize inadvertently, and *finden*, to find ; analogous is *flottweg schaffen*, to procure smartly, which is a pun on *flott wegschaffen*, to make away with gaily ; *klaufen*, to seclude, as neat a euphemism as I have seen ; and *auf Gemüsetour gehen*, to make a tour of the vegetables, a phrase closely allied to *reconnoitre* but only roughly equivalent to the Tommy's *to scrounge about*, which, signifying to seek an opportunity for ' removing ' either a particular article or whatever chance may offer, derives from *to scrounge*, transitive and intransitive, to steal, to procure by dubious means—such a development from dialect as is often considered to form one of the corner-stones of soldiers' slang, another being *wangle* (pre-War but enfranchised by the Tommy), ' to procure goods or an advantage illicitly but without punishment, by the exercise of cunning, moral pressure, [bluff,] blackmail or bribery ' (Brophy). The French have a wealth of synonyms—nearly twice as many as the British, who in their turn have twice as many as the Germans. *Anglaiser*, ' to English ', to remove, to steal, provides an interesting comment ; *se procurer, système dé*, from *débrouillard*, a handy man ; *faire aux as*, where *as* is pre-War Parisian argot for money ; *asphyxier* ; *balancer*, where the semantic progression is to balance, to throw (*parce qu'on balance le bras avant de lancer un objet au loin*, Dauzat), to throw away with a view to finding later, to find later, to remove ; *camoufler*, a development from the original and the militarily technical senses of to camouflage ; *chaparder, choper* and *chipoter*, attenuations ; euphemisms such as *balayer* and *faucher, emprunter* and *tomber faible sur, grouper, chauffer* ; old locutions or terms such as *rouper* (anciently *roupiner*) and *prendre à la foire d'empoigne*, to get at the fair of take-as-you-please ; brutalities like *étouffer*, to stifle, and *voracer*, to wolf ; military words like *razzier*, to raid, *embusquer*, and *mobiliser* ; energeticisms like *s'emballer sur*, to go ' bald-headed ' for, *se faire les crochets sur* or *se casser les poignets sur*, to get one's hands on at any price ; *payer*, or *payer le prix courant*, pay a non-existent price, the sum being assessed by the Poilu at the precise amount of *trois francs cinq sous*, which looks like a sly hit at French bureaucracy ; *rabioter*, to take what one hopes is superfluous, to scrounge— Déchelette has a charming ' essayette ' on the word ; *ratatiner*, to shrivel up ; *secouer une chemise* (Dauzat : ' *l'objet est tombé tout seul !* ') ; *travailler*, to work, i.e. to procure something by working for it, much like our colloquial *work it* ; *faisander*, a fanciful development of *faire* or *faire aux pattes*, which is thieves' slang for to steal. English synonyms from thieves' slang or, at the best, from low slang, are *make*, which dates from the late seventeenth century for to steal, soldiers using it chiefly in the senses, to acquire illicitly, to borrow forgetfully; *nab*, older still, with a connotation of speed; *lift*, likewise from the sixteenth century; *bone*, from the eighteenth century, as is *snaffle* (cf. *snaffler*, a highwayman); *nick*, from a century earlier, as indeed is *win*, of which the 1914–18 neologistic counterpart is *earn*, both phrases stressing not only a circuitous illegality but also, subconsciously no doubt, the rightness of the taker's course; and *pinch*, nineteenth century, with the rhyming variant *half-inch*. Other English synonyms are *(to)souvenir*, a War coinage either for to remove without asking permission yet hardly with criminal intention, or for to search for *and* find; *hotstuff*, to appropriate illicitly, to steal, whence *hotstuffer*, a man given to promiscuous borrowings and dubious removings, and *swipe*, a Canadianism equivalent to *hotstuff*.

In all these groups of words, and indeed in any other relevant group whatsoever, one sees that while the combatants experience a sharp and vivid reaction and promptly respond to the vitally changed conditions and to the need for new words and phrases or for old words and phrases twisted in form and regarmented in meaning, those men also, instead of constantly and consistently dwelling on the change, hark back to the security, homeliness, comfort, quiet and liberty of peace. The old vocabulary not merely subserves the demands of the new, but often it is so inwoven with the new that one has to relate the War-time word or phrase to the War itself: one has, in fact, to put oneself in the place of the soldiers. Otherwise, these domestic or vocational terms would mean only what they meant before the War : such terms have been the quickest to disappear from general speech. It is the War-mintings (new either in form or, far more often, in sense only) which have worn best ; many of these have become incorporated in the normal spoken language ; some few have even achieved rights of literary citizenship. But, much more important, those writers who have been through the War (and even those who have merely mixed freely with the survivors) have acquired a hatred for sham, hesitancy, pretentiousness, high-falutin, pomposity, verbosity and verbiage ; some of these have gone too far, their influence has done much to destroy the ample, the rhythmical, the musical prose that once was generally recognized to be no less English than the terser, abrupter style that has always been considered typically 'Saxon'. There are, however, signs that the pendulum has begun to swing the other way ; that movement will be all to the good, if only the salutary, war-taught lesson of directness, vigour, simplicity, modesty, true realism and stark sincerity be not forgotten.

APPENDIX I

BOXING DAY

IN its frequently humorous fashion, the great 'Oxford Dictionary' defines Boxing Day as 'the first week-day after Christmas-Day, observed as a holiday on which postmen, errand-boys, and servants of various kinds expect to receive a Christmas-box', and certainly those who are so lucky as to be able to expect (rather than those whose hearts sink as they realize that they are expected to give) Christmas-boxes do not consider a Sunday as, technically, Boxing Day.

Originally a Christmas-box was a receptacle (usually of earthenware) set aside for the tips of servants, apprentices and other dependants; into this the moneys were put during the year, and after Christmas, generally the first day after, this receptacle was broken open and the contents shared. Hence *Boxing Day*. In Sweden the Christmas-box is called *julklapp* (i.e. jul-klapp, Yule-clap), a knock on the door at Yuletide or, as we say nowadays, at Christmastide. That is the real origin of Boxing Day; if anyone should set his eyes on, he should not be misled by, a statement that appears in the 1884 Christmas Number of 'Harper's Magazine': 'In consequence of the multiplicity of business on Christmas-day, the giving of

Christmas-boxes was postponed to the 26th, St. Stephen's Day, which became the established Boxing-Day.' They do so love their little joke across the Herring Pond!

Of St. Stephen's Day there is a famous proverbial couplet, now forgotten—or never heard—by most of us:

> Blessed be St. Stephen,
> There is no fast upon his even.

Another folk-lore rhyme has a very practical application:

> If you bleed your nag on St. Stephen's Day,
> He'll work your work for ever and aye.

St. Stephen's Day was the date at which medieval, Elizabethan and Stuart Englishmen bled their horses. The practice was observed by all ranks of people, and Thomas Tusser in his rough but lively poem, 'The Five Hundred Points of Good Husbandry' (1557), says:

Ere Christmas [i.e. Christmastide] be past, let horse be let blood,
For many a purpose it doth him much good;
The day of St. Stephen our fathers did use;
If that do displease thee, some other day choose.

This practice was perhaps introduced into England by the Danes. According to a very early writer, the procedure was to gallop the horses 'into a lather' and then bleed them. The great antiquarian, John Aubrey, mentions this being done regularly in the next century. On the 26th December, even the Pope's stud horses were physicked and bled. St. Stephen being the patron saint of the turf—or at least of horses.

APPENDIX II

SOME GROUPS OF 'TOMMY' WORDS

FROM the army slang words of 1914–18 one may form certain groups that are particularly reminiscent of the trials and humours of the times; certain terms, certain phrases, smelling still of earth and fear, filth and eager experience.

It is true that there was much of *camouflage* and *eyewash*, but they had their funny side. The official definition of *camouflage* is 'the art of concealing that something is concealed'. Little heard before 1917, it derives from French slang *camoufler*, to disguise; on March 5th of that year G. B. Shaw wrote in one of the daily newspapers: 'I was in khaki by way of camouflage.' It soon came to mean deception, and could be used as a verb: 'Here's Corporal Jones, camouflaged as a soldier!' *Eyewash*, perhaps —in its slang sense—from the United States, was a useful variation on the frenchified word, and was used to indicate sham or humbug, flattery, deceit, pretentiousness, ostentation designed to hide an ugly fact or some deplorable desideratum.

One kind of *eyewash*, the army's innumerable 'states' and 'returns', was known as *bumf*, short for *bumfodder*: the abbreviation was common in English public schools from before 1900; the full term for toilet-paper dates back to the seventeenth century, when it was coined by Urquhart, the translator of Rabelais; Urquhart is one of the most prolific originators of the obscenities and vulgarisms of our language, and with him rank Shakespeare and Burns. The proper 'stage' for the use of bumf was the *jakes*, etymology doubtful; but perhaps the word, as the O.E.D. suggests, represents *Jack's house, place*, and it has been in use for at least four hundred years. The official name was *latrine*, from Latin *latrina*, a lavatory. The rumours that flew about so gaily were often called *latrine rumours*, more vulgarly *s——house rumours*; less offensively they were known as *transport tales, cook-house yarns, shaves* (old Regular Army), or, among the Australians, *furphies*, from *Furphy*, a relevant contractor at Melbourne. The naval equivalents are *cook-house official, cook's-galley yarn, forecastle wireless* (post-war), and *galley-packet*. The activity of the cooks is obvious.

Jakes reminds us of two curious terms of assent: *jake* and *jake-a-loo*. Colonial troops employed them thus: 'It's jake *or* jake-a-loo', it's correct, genuine, true, no hoax. The origin is unknown. Another odd term of assent was *jannock*, of Scandinavian origin, but in widespread use in English dialect for fair, 'straight', 'square', honest; the earlier record in 'The English Dialect Dictionary' is for 1841, but the O.E.D. takes us back to 1828. Often spelt and pronounced *jonnick* or *jonnuck*, and sometimes serving as an adverb. 'It's jannock' or 'that's jannock' means 'that's all right', 'that's honest', 'good enough to act on'.

Dissent was frequently indicated by the use of *Fanny Adams* in some form or other. The phrase is a puzzle.

SOME GROUPS OF 'TOMMY' WORDS

Fanny Adams is the naval equivalent for *Harriet Lane*, used of any preserved meat. Harriet Lane was murdered in the 1870's; the culprit was hanged and then 'housed' at Madame Tussaud's in 'The Chamber of Horrors'. Fanny Adams was murdered about 1812. Both of these young women were cut up; hence the grim naval slang. From the navy, doubtless, came the amplification *sweet Fanny Adams*, a term that, after meaning 'something of little value', took on the sense of 'nothing'. 'He knew sweet Fanny Adams about his job' might have been heard in the army prior to the War. In 1914–18 it served as a euphemism for *sweet f—— all*, itself freemasoned into *sweet F.A.* or coded into *F.A.*. It is, however, uncertain whether the *sweet F.A.* and *F.A.* forms originally derived from *Fanny Adams* and caught the infection of the uglier phrase, or whether the *Fanny Adams* form was enlisted to tone down, to serve as a polite variant of, that ugly expletive. 'What did the quartermaster give you?' 'Sweet F.A.'

Down in their *dug-outs*, the men could laugh at their misfortunes. That word was also applied (first about 1900, I believe) to elderly officers returning to service or to officers that had long had a 'cushy' job. The men usually had mere funk-holes, small cavities or 'cupboards' below the parapet or, unwisely, the parados; no disparagement to the occupants is, or ever was, intended by the word, which was occasionally used in the Boer War. Likewise, it was not a disgrace for a man *to have the wind up*, but *windy* meant habitually frightened and could be employed as a pejorative. *Wind vertical* came late, and was rather an officers' elaboration. *To get the wind up* is not wholly a post-war variant that can be applied to mere nervousness, for it appears in the writings of several war correspondents in 1916–18. *To put the wind up* marks a development from *have the wind up*.

Extreme *wind up*, prolonged beyond the nerves' endurance, sometimes ended in madness. The following adjectives signify ' mad ' in some degree or other. *Batchy* is mad, or merely silly ; etymology extremely doubtful. *Batty* almost certainly (*batchy* just possibly) comes from *bats in the belfry*, and the rhyming *scatty* is related to the Derbyshire *scattle* (easily frightened) and the obsolete Yorkshire *scatterling* (a heedless person) ; both *batty* and *scatty* mean quite mad. *Crackers*, as in ' he's crackers ' or ' he's gone crackers ', links up with *cracked*, a little mad or quite mad. *Dingo*, slightly insane, derives from the French slang *dingot*, eccentric, mad. *Dippy* and *loopy*, properly *looby*, are highly expressive ; *looby* is very old indeed, appearing in Langland's ' Piers Plowman ', 1377, when it denoted lazy, though later it came to signify stupid, the final transition to silly, a little mad, being an easy one. *Dippy* is temporarily insane or only stupid or even momentarily slow-witted : perhaps from *dipsomaniac*. From India we have *doolally*, mad, from Deolali, famous in the Regular Army, and a variation was *doolally tap*, where *tap*, Hindustani for fever, may have been influenced by *tapped*, also used for ' mad ', one whose brains have been ' tapped '. India gives us the less used *piache*, mad, very rarely heard outside of Regulars with Indian service ; on the analogy of *stone mad*, *stone piache* was employed for a change. Like *piache*, *poggle* or *puggle* arose in India, and was an old army word. Egypt presented us with *maghnoon*,

SOME GROUPS OF 'TOMMY' WORDS

properly a dolt, but meaning slightly mad. *In Ponkey Land* was congenitally silly or weak-witted, and only rarely did it find itself used for madness. *Touched* was originally touched with the sun (as also, in fact, was *doolally*) or perhaps *touched in one's mind* or *brain* or *wits*, where *touched* is 'tainted', 'spoilt'. *Winick* or *stone winick* (*to be* or *to go*) denoted extreme foolishness, or slight or temporary insanity : Winick in Lancashire has a lunatic asylum. So have other towns.

Slightly more cheerful are the two most popular adaptation-adoptions from French : *napoo* and *san fairy ann*. The former equals *il n'y en a plus*, there is no more, and it was corrupted—or enriched (opinions differ)—to convey 'finished', 'empty', 'gone', even 'dead'; I have also heard it used as a verb : 'That bleeder's napoo'd the rum !' *San fairy ann* represents *ça ne fait rien*, a colloquialism for *cela n'a aucune importance*, that doesn't matter, never mind ! The phrase was often shortened to *San Fairy*, elaborated to *San Fairy Anna*, or debased—though this was rarer—to *Aunt Mary Ann*.

Even from detention and imprisonment could the Tommy and his Colonial peers extract occasional amusement. For prison or detention or field punishment, or for two or all the three of these, the following terms were in use among 'the troops' in 1914–18 : *Birdcage* and *cage, boob, chokey, clink, cold storage, cooler, coop, hutch, jankers, jug, moosh* or *mush, nick, Paddy Doyle, quod* ; *limbered* = placed under arrest, and so does *jugged*, while *to be jugged* = to be in cells ; *seven penn'orth* = seven days' confinement to barracks ; *Bow Street* = the orderly room ; *on the peg* = awaiting trial.

Some of these words deserve more than so cursory a mention. *Birdcage* was usually applied to the enclosure in which, previous to their departure for prison camps in the rear, prisoners of war were effectually constrained behind the barbed wire. A war-coinage in this sense; but *cage*, for prison, dates back to about 1590, appears in Dr. Johnson's Dictionary in 1755, and deteriorated to slang and then to cant, that picturesque and doubly-intriguing lingo spoken by the criminal and vagabond classes. *Boob* for either a military prison or a guard-room is an Americanism. *Chokey*, also spelt *choky* and *chokee*, comes from India. *Clink* was used of the famous prison in Southwark (S.E. London) as early as 1515, and probably a good deal earlier. *Cold storage* and *cooler* are obviously associate words. *Coop* is short for *hen-coop*, and *hutch* for *rabbit-hutch*. *Jankers*, which meant either the cells or the punishment meted out to defaulters (hence also the bugle-call that summoned them to report), is probably a very old word, but its misty story has defied plausible explanation. *Jug* abbreviates *stone-jug*, a late eighteenth-century cant term, as were its variants *stone-doublet* and *stone-tavern*—the navy discovering *stone-frigate* about 1800. *Mush* may derive from the dialect verb so spelt and meaning ' to beat cruelly; to subdue or break the spirit of anyone by harsh treatment ' (to quote from Wright's invaluable ' English Dialect Dictionary '), which has existed for a century or more. *Paddy Doyle* is a regular-army word, meaning ' defaulters '; to do *Paddy Doyle* means to be a defaulter. *Quod* is over two hundred years old, and may have been suggested by the quadrangle of a prison. *Clink, jug,* and *quod* were also used as verbs

SOME GROUPS OF 'TOMMY' WORDS

(to imprison); *limbered* may be an army corruption and elaboration of *limbo*, old slang for a prison, and prompted by the theological phrase *in limbo patrum*. The ancient cant *nabbed*, arrested, survived to 1914–18, and after.

Most military cells and prisons were infested with lice (Grose in 1785 has the synonyms: gentleman's companion, a louse), variously known as *chatts*, *coots*, *crabs*, *grey-backs*, *live-stock*. The fourth name, specific for the kind so described, is of uncertain date, and *crabs* is short for *crab-lice* (recorded in Grose). *Chat*, *chatt*, *chate*, is the oldest of these five words: it occurs in B.E.'s ' Dictionary of the Canting Crew ', published at some date in the period 1690–1700, and it originated as cant: Grose is probably right in conjecturing ' an abbreviation of chattels ', such goods as one carries or can carry about with one. *Coot* is of uncertain date and origin. *Live-stock*, dialect and slang, in the eighteenth century denoted either lice or fleas. The most frequent adjectives were *chatty*, *cooty*, and *crummy*, of which the last is Regular Army, from cant of unascertained remoteness; it is perhaps a sense-distortion of the *crummy* defined by Dyche, in the fifth edition of his Dictionary, 1748, as ' full of crumb; also fat, rich, plump, or fleshy '. Less often heard were these: *Bosom chums*; *chicot*, verminous, probably a French approximation to *hitchy koo*, sometimes used by the Tommy in this sense; *dimback*, a louse; *seam-squirrel*, a fanciful word rarely employed by the ' other ranks '; *ticky*, lousy; *toto*, a louse, was originally a French army slang word, *gau* or *got* being equally favoured by the Poilu. For a charming essay on the war louse of 1914–18, see François Déchelette's

'L'Argot des Poilus', which is the best of the three excellent dictionaries of French soldiers' slang.

But one could go far towards forgetting the trenches, the 'crimes', and the lice if one had plenty of money. We may, therefore, end on a happy note by mentioning a few of the army's slang words for this essential of so much material enjoyment. *Compo* meant either pay or money, and it was taken over from nautical slang: in 1901 it was defined by John S. Farmer as 'a sailor's term for his monthly advance of wages'. *Dough* was heard much more frequently; it cannot be found in such representative and comprehensive lexicographers as Hotten, Farmer, Joseph Wright, Weekley, the Oxford editors: from which I gather that it either belongs to, or only slightly antedates, the war years. *Onks*, properly francs, would occasionally be heard as a loose equivalent to 'money'. *Oscar*, money, is short for Oscar Asche (the famous Australian actor), rhyming slang for *cash*, and dating from about 1910; *rhino*, somehow connected with *rhinoceros* and usually preceded by the adjective *ready*, has meant money, especially cash, since the late seventeenth century. *Snow*, an old cant term for silver, came to mean money, and so the soldiers mostly used it. *Sugar*, needing no explanation, is nearly a century old.

APPENDIX III

THE *POILU* ON HIMSELF AND OTHERS

THE names given by any nation to all other nations are interesting, often amusing, and always revelatory of the originator's character in general and of its national attitude at the moment. Still more significant, considerably more significant, than the nicknames bestowed by civilians, the majority of whom take their opinions ready-made from the Press, are the names by which any national army refers to all other soldiers, whether allied or opponent.

Our English colloquial and argotic designations of foreign soldiers are fairly well known, even in England, but the picturesque terms employed by the French troops for their Allies and for ' the Huns ' form an almost closed book. As the Frenchman would himself admit, we cannot begin better than with his names for himself. Much the best known in England is *poilu*, the hairy one, a man's man, a thoroughly stout fellow ; but while a French officer might say ' I want six poilus for the ration-party ', a non-com. or a private would use the word only in the sense of mate, pal, companion. In fact, while a civilian rarely said anything else for *soldat*, the soldier himself tended to avoid the word, largely because the *ciblots* or ' civvies ' so used it and in part because the newspapers took it up with such sickening unction. The official term, i.e. the Army word, for the soldier was *l'homme*, the man. The unofficial Army words were *bonshommes* and *gars*, ' good men ' and ' fellows ', unless indeed they were the slangy *type*, individual, and *mec*, chap ; *type* has passed into general French slang, *mec* has remained thieves' slang ; this latter word originated among the Apaches of Paris and is now heard occasionally in decent circles for *macro*, a ' bully ' ; like so many other low argotic words, *mec* in the army lost its unsavoury associations but, on being demobilized, it returned, with a change, to its evil ways, in much the same fashion as the English *win*, to steal.

The Poilu's name for the Belgian soldier was *piote* ; so too did ' the Belgies ' speak of themselves. Before the War it was French cavalry slang for an infantryman. The Italian, by the Poilu as by the Tommy, was mostly called *Macaroni* ; sometimes, by abbreviation, *Talien* ; during the War *Italboche*, so popular in the 'nineties and in the first decade of the present century, was rarely heard. *Talien* came from Serbia. The Serbians were called *Serbos*, just as the Greeks were called *Grécos* (*o* was a very common suffix among the Poilus) ; but sometimes the Serbians were named *Dobros*, this being the Serbian word for ' good ' and recurring in their conversation as often as *bon* does in that of a Frenchman. Russians became *Ruskis*, *Russkis*, *Rousskis*, and *Rousses*, much as the Tommy called them ' Russky ' or ' Ivan '. The Bulgarians were *Bubuls*, or *Bougres* from the medieval form of the word, or *Boulg* as an abbreviation of the still older form *Boulgres* from the Latin *Bulgari*.

The German, whether soldier or civilian, was called

Boche, which English journalists and then ordinary Englishmen adopted; in both languages as either noun or adjective. *Boche*, a much discussed word, is probably the unfavourable suffix *boche* that we have already seen in *Italboche*; it is at least established that *Alleboche* was very commonly used for *Allemand* before *Boche* became so popular; but it has not yet been proved whether *boche* is a shortening of *Alleboche* or whether the latter form was suggested by the long-established term *tête de boche*, an obstinate (or a stupidly obstinate) fellow or, in less select circles, a bad lot. More interesting is the fact that a famous French marshal used *Boche* even though certain high officials hated the word being honoured with admission into the sacrosanct vocabulary of bureaucracy. Very often, however, the Poilu spoke of 'Jerry' as *Fritz*, which, by the way, was the commonest English form in 1914–16; but the Poilu used it far more often of *any* German than we did. On the other hand, he sometimes referred to 'Jerry' as *Friedrick*, which, so far as I know, we never did. In 1918 the French soldier might use *Frigolin*. More common than either of the two names last mentioned was *Pointu*, from the pointed helmet worn by the German infantryman; as early as 1916, however, the word was applied to any German whatsoever. The German artilleryman was often alluded to as *Otto, Ernest, Michel*. Of the three best French lexicographers of the slang of the poilu, Dauzat, Déchelette and Esnault, only the last-named cites *Ya* and *Ya-Ya*; from *ja*, the German for 'yes'.

The *Ya-Ya* kind of nickname reminds me that, walking down a Paris boulevard in January 1918, I was accosted by an American soldier, who wanted nothing more expensive than a match; he thanked me and added: 'I can't make these gardam Dee-Donks understand me.' That was the first occasion on which I had heard the French called *Dee-Donks*; it comes from *dis donc!*, an expression as common to a Frenchman as *say!* is to an American; and that further reminds me that Australian soldiers sometimes alluded to the American troops as 'those goddam say-guys!' All three sobriquets may be paralleled by *Oh la la*, the name given by very many German and some American soldiers to the French, more especially to the soldier than the civilian. I once heard an old 'swaddy' exclaim: 'When I tried to make up to that Froggie bint, she only said *oh! la la!*' As others see us . . .

The Poilu occasionally spoke of 'the Doughboys' (the name-elect of the American soldiers) as *Ricains* just as he had earlier decided to call the Italians *Taliens*. Like the Tommy, he also called them *Yanks*: but with less of depreciation. *Teddies* (from Theodore Roosevelt) never gained much ground in France despite the efforts of her newspapers; nor was it at all common in the British Army, which preferred *Sammy*. *Sammy*, like *Teddy*, was unpopular in the United States, but it caught on with the Poilu, who, like Tommy, practically never used *Doughboy*.

None of these French nicknames for the American soldier was half so general as *Tommy*, *Tommies* for the English soldier. As Kipling had popularized the word in England, so several of the leading Parisian journalists launched and familiarized the word in France; but it is to be noted that, similarly to *Poilu*,

THE POILU

Tommy was much less used at the Front than among civilians. *Khakis* or *Kakis*, as a name for Tommy, is not even mentioned by delightful Déchelette or by erudite Esnault; Dauzat, recognizing its rarity among the Poilus, notes that it was a War coinage from the colour of the British uniform. Esnault observes that *khaki*, as the name of a dress-material, so far lost its original meaning as to be employed of another colour, as in *un uniforme de khaki bleu*; compare *à cheval sur un âne*. Far more than *Khaki*, *Angliche* was the name for a British soldier; but as before and since the War, *Angliche* fitted a civilian as well as a soldier, a female of any age as well as man or boy. In pre-War days it was definitely not used by the leisured, nor by the professional classes: now it may come from the lips of the most cultured or the most aristocratic: evidently it is not merely a corruption of *English* but the obvious French pronunciation of a very un-Gallic sound.

It may be remarked that while the Poilu had no nickname for the Canadian soldier, he—or at least the French artilleryman—was in 1918 wont to call the 1918 conscripts *canadiens* because in 1915–17 the French artillery had many Canadian horses, which were difficult to handle: so were the 1918 conscripts. Nor had the Poilu a name for the South African soldiers. But *Anzac* was, after 1915, a familiar French journalistic word for the Australian or the New Zealand soldier; the name 'took' well with the French civilian but only moderately with the French soldier.

In conclusion, it may not be amiss to record the Tommies' nicknames for the Poilu: *Poilu* itself; *Piou-Piou*, a very old French Regular Army word discarded in France during the War save occasionally as a synonym for *pousse-caillou*, 'pebble-pusher', the equivalent of our 'foot-slogger'; far more generally, *Frenchy*; and most popular of all, *Frog* or *Froggie*, as in 'Them Frogs are bloody good over the top (i.e. in a charge), but they don't hang on like us silly b——s'.

INDEX

acorn, 126
Adversary, the, 16, 18
Ainsworth, Harrison, 145
All Fools' Day, 60–5
American slang: comments, instances, 9, 28–9, 48, 72–8, 203, 216, 222
Angliche, 223
Anzac, 223
Aubrey, 210
Australian slang: comments, examples, 9, 27–8, 70, 212, 222

Bache, Richard, 98
back slang, 31, 35–8
bad bargain, 126, 136
Bailey, N., 108, 113
Balzac, 150
barbaque, 173, 193
Barbey d'Aurevilly, 191
Barbusse, 175, 176, 191
Barham, 152, 195
Bartlett, lexicographer, 98
Bauche, Henri, 93
bayonet in soldiers' slang, 186–7
B.E., lexicographer, 4, 26, 43, 52, 139, 140, 145, 217
beak, beck, 136–7
Beard, John R., 16
beaver, bever, 49–51
Beelzebub, 19
beetle-crusher, 146
Besant, Sir Walter, 79
bess, betty; jemmy, 127
binge, 137
Bischoff, Dr. Erich, 181
bite, 48

biting-on, 47, 48
Blackacre, Whiteacre, 68–9
Blackstone, 66
bleeding, 83–4
blinking, 84
bloody, 79–90
blooming, 79, 84
bluet, 163–4
blurry, 84
bo, 23, 28
Boche, 168, 186, 221
bone, to, 138, 206
Borrow, 25
Boswell, 44, 114
Botrel, T., 163
Bowen, Frank C., 5, 137, 142–3, 147, 149
Boxing Day, 209–10
Bradley, Henry, 113
Brophy, John, 34, 84, 137–52 *passim*, 182, 204
brown George, 142
Browning, R., 44
buddy, 23, 28–9
Bullokar, 107
bumf, 211
bums, 76
bundook, 185
burgoo, 141
Burke, James P., 72
Burne's 'Folk-Lore', 54
Burns, 19, 21, 48, 78, 124–5, 212
Butler, S. ('Hudibras'), 147

cafard, 177
cage, 144, 216
cagna, 170, 192
camerade, 147

225

camouflage, 211
Canadien, 223
cant (thieves' slang), 11, 36–9 *passim*, 136–47 *passim*, 181, 184, 204–6 *passim*, 217, 218
canting, 127
capout, kapout, 147, 178, 180, 196
Carlyle, 84
Carnoy, Prof., 93–7
carol, 57
Carus, Paul, 16
centre slang, 31, 38–9
'Century Dictionary', 113–14
Chalkers, 127
'Chambers's Twentieth Century Dictionary', 49, 113
chat(t), 217
Chaucer, 139
Chesterfield, 116–17
china, 34, 78
Christmas, philology of, 53–9
Christmas Boxes, 58, 209–10
chum, 23, 24, 25–6, 143
cigars in German soldiers' slang, 160
click, to, 143–4
clink, 144, 216
cobber, 23, 27–8, 143
Cockeram, 107
Cockney, 30, 32, 36
Coe, novelist, 73
coffin-nail, 160
Coke, 69
cold-meal ticket, 152
collector, 13
'Concise Oxford Dictionary', 43, 44, 48, 49, 113
Congreve, 22
Cooper's 'Thesaurus', 51
cop, 151–2, 194
Cotgrave, 45
Craigie, Sir Wm., 113, 114
Creech, 26
crummy, 217
cushy, 169, 213

damper, 47
Dana, 82, 149
Dauzat, 162–7, 177, 180, 205, 223

death in War slang, 195–7
decent, 79
Déchelette, F., 147, 162–7, 180, 190, 203, 205, 217–18
Defoe, 12, 17, 151
demon, 17–18
De Quincey, 41
deuce, 22
Devil, the, 16–22
dialect, 42–51 *passim*
dickens, the, 21–2
digger, 23, 27
Dobrée, Bonamy, 117
dodge the column, 145, 199–200
doggy, 47
Dorgelès, 196
double Dutch, 5–6
dough, 218
Dough-Boy, 222
drunk, 95, 176
Dryden, 11, 43, 81
dug-out, synonyms, 191–2, 213
D'Urfey, 22
Dutch, 3, 5–6, 9
Dutch courage, 3, 6
Dyche, Thomas, 39, 138, 217

Edgeworth, Maria, 47
elevener, elevens, 48–9
Eliot, George, 44
Enemy, the, 18
English, pejorative, 7, 8
enthusiast, 110
Epps, J., 16
Ersatz, 178, 180
Esnault, G., 162–7, 172, 175, 176, 181, 188, 198, 221, 223
Etherege, 81
Eumenides, 91
euphemism and euphemisms, 91–102
every inch, 151
eye-wash, 211

Fanny Adams, 212–13
Farmer and Henley, 29, 43, 47, 82, 100, 139, 143, 218
Farrar, Dean, 67
fasting in French slang, 175

INDEX

fear in soldiers' slang, 201–2
fellow, 24
fiend, 18
Florio, 45
Foote, 82
footpads, 10–15
footslogger, 189
foot-wabbler, 145–6
Fowlers, lexicographers and grammarians, 91, 111, 112, 164
Fraser and Gibbons, 27, 49, 142–3, 156, 181
French, pejorative, 3, 6–7
French cream, 128
French leave, 3, 7
Fritz, 157, 171, 221
Frog(gy), 222, 224
Front-pig, 156
Funk and Wagnalls, 113
funk-hole, 191

Garçon, M., 16
Gaskell, Mrs., 10–11
gentleman commoner, 128
German, pejorative, 3, 7
German duck, 7
Gerry, Jerry, 148, 184, 221
gibberish, 39–40
go west, 152–3, 197
Goethe, 17, 160
Gosse, Edmund, 115–16
Gower, 71
Graf, A., 16
Graff and Borman, 156, 181–2
Greek, pejorative, 3–4
Greenough and Kittredge, 24, 92
Grose, Capt. Francis, 4, 6, 7, 9, 12, 13, 24, 26, 32, 39, 43, 46, 47, 52, 63, 67, 88, 122–31, 137–52 *passim*, 217
grouse, 146
Grub Street, 128–9
guts, 146

Hans Wurst, 180
Harman, 136
haversack in soldiers' slang, 188
Hexham, Henry, 51
highwaymen, 10–15

hobo, 28, 76
Hood, 101
Hotten, J. C., 12, 24, 30, 33, 35, 36, 39, 40, 49, 82, 100, 101, 139, 142, 146, 218
Howitt, 48
Hughes, T., 151
huile de coudre, 65
Hun, Hunnish, 7

imprisonment in soldiers' slang, 202–4, 215–16
Indian up, get one's, 9
infantryman in slang, 145–6, 156, 189–90
Inge, Dean, 86
Irish, pejorative, 9
Irish beauty, 9, 129
Irwin, Godfrey, 28, 29, 72, 74, 76, 77, 78

Jäger, 156
jakes, 212
jam, 147
jankers, 144, 203, 216
jannock, 212
jerry, to, 78
jippo, 141–2
John-a-Nokes, Tom-a-Stiles, 67–8, 69
John Doe, Richard Roe, 66–7, 69
Johnson, Dr., 26, 107, 108, 109, 112, 113–21, 144, 164, 216
Jonson, Ben, 6
jug, stone-jug, 144–5, 203, 216
Julot, 170, 171
junk, 75–6
junker, junk-hound, 75

kaka, 174
kamerad(e), 147, 169, 179
Karachos, 178, 179
Karo, 159
Kersey, John, 108
Kingsley, H., 29
kip, 147–8
Kipling, 147
knight, 14
Kriegs- compounds, 180

Lamb, 17
landowner, become a, 151, 152
Langland, 214
Latitudinarian, 110
Lenôtre, G., 164
lice in soldiers' slang, 159, 164, 170, 188, 217-18
limbered, 217
Limey, 77
lingo, 129
Lingua Franca, 129, 191, 196
looby, loopy, 214
loony, 100
Lord of Misrule, 58
Lucifer, 18
lunch, luncheon, 44-5

machine-gun in French soldiers' slang, 170, 172-3
— in German soldiers' slang, 159
Mackay, C., 83, 87
McKnight, Prof. G., 92, 94
mad, 100, 214-15
Mahoun, 19
make, 138, 206
man in the street, the, 70
Mansfield, 40-1, 50
Marlowe, 17
marmalade in German soldiers' slang, 159-60
Marryat, 99
Marston, 81
Masefield, 81, 82
mate, 23-4, 143
Matthews, J. Brander, 84
mec, 220
meestle, 78
Mencken, 85, 86, 87, 92, 98, 99, 101
Methodist, 110
mile-eater, 156
Milton, 17, 20
Minsheu, 51, 107, 112
Montague, C. E., 85
Moore, T., 152
Morris's 'Austral English', 28, 47, 70, 143
moukère, 168

Murray, Sir James, 12-13, 26, 113
mush, 216

nab, 138-9, 217
nacket, nocket, 46
nail, to, 138, 139
Napier, 149
napoo, 197, 215
natal, 56
necking, 77
nice, 79
Niceforo, A., 92-3
Nick, 19-20
no man's land, 151, 192
Noel, 55-6
nuncheon, 44-6

offensive nationality, 3-9
old = wicked, 19-21
old boots, 20
old man, the, 158, 199
old soldier, 148-9, 200
on the spot, 76
Onions, Dr., 112, 113
Orrery, 149
Oscar (money), 218
over the top, 149, 193
'Oxford English Dictionary', 3, 6, 11, 26, 29, 35, 40, 43, 46, 47, 49, 69, 81, 82, 87, 100, 113, 114, 137-53 *passim*, 209, 218

pack, 148
Packard, novelist, 73
pad, 11-12
paddy, 9
padre, 136
pal, 13, 23, 24-5, 143
'Paston Letters', 51
pempe, 65
petits pois, 170
Phillips, Edward, 108
philology, 110
piece, 47, 48
pinch, to, 139, 206
pineapple, 77
Piote, 220
Platt, J., 53

INDEX

'Pocket Oxford Dictionary', 111–12
Poilu, 157, 171, 219, 223
poisson d'avril, 62
pop, 14
Pope, A., 43
pousse-caillou, 146, 189
pozzy, 140–1
'Promptorium Parvulorum', 23, 51
prostitution, euphemisms, 101
push, 149
push up daisies, 153, 195

queer, 14, 129
quod, 144, 145, 216

racket, 74
Raleigh, Prof. Sir Walter, 114
Ray, John, 51–2
representative names, 66–71
rhino, 218
rhyming slang, 30–5, 78, 192, 218
Richardson, 82
rifle in soldiers' slang, 185–6
ripping, 79
romantic, 110
Romany, 13, 25, 29, 78
Rosalie, 163, 171, 187
ruffian, 19
rum, 14
rumours in soldiers' slang, 201–2, 212
Ruskin, 82

Sala, G. A., 150
san fairy ann, 215
Satan, 15, 18
scamp, 14–15
scanties, 99
Scotch, pejorative, 9
Scott, 58, 78, 149
scout, 130
scran, 142, 188
scrounge, 139–40, 204
Seccombe, T., 115
Shakespeare, 14, 21, 71, 144, 148, 151, 212
shave-tail, 77–8

Shaw, G. B., 80, 82, 85, 211
Shaw, T. E., 141
shelling in military slang, 197–8
Shelta, 13
'Shorter Oxford Dictionary', 101
show, 149–50
Sidney, Sir Philip, 68
singe (in French), 174
Skeat, 53, 67
Skinner's 'Etymologicon', 113
Smith, Alexander, 71
Smith, Capt. Alex., 10
Smith, L. Pearsall, 42, 79, 117–18
smoke, 74–5
Smollett, 7, 22
snack, 42–3
snaffle, 14, 140, 206
snap, 44
snow, 218
soldiers' slang, English, 31–2, 135–53, 211–18 ; *passim* 181–207
—— French, 147, 150, 162–80, 219–24 ; *passim* 181–207
—— German, 146, 154–61 ; *passim* 181–207
sorry, *surry*, 26–7
Spanish, pejorative, 3, 5
Spanish coin, 5
Spanish trumpet, 5
Spenser, 148
spiflicate, 130
spurlos versenkt, 180
stealing in soldiers' slang, 138–40, 204–6
steel-helmet in slang, 187–8
Stendhal, 196
Stevens, Capt. John, 43, 45, 52
Stevens, G. A., 68
strafe, 169, 179, 198
sugar, 218
swaddy, 151
Sweet, 53
Swift, 22, 127–8, 147
swing the lead, 145

tacot, 171
tape, to, 148
tarantula, 111

Teddy, 222
Tempter, the, 18
ten-o'clock, 48
Thackeray, 7, 22
tiffin, 46
Tilsley, W. V., 85
tin-hat, 187
toby, 12-13
Tom, Dick and Harry, 70-1
tommy, 142-3
Tommy Atkins, 150, 222-3
tooth-pick, 159, 187
toto, 217
tramps, 72-3, 76
Trench, R. C., 42
truc, 192
tulip of the storm, 158, 187
Turk, pejorative, 3-4
Tusser, 44, 210
twelve-hours, 48, 49
Tyndale, 18

Uhlan, 157
'Universal Dictionary of the English Language', 43, 44, 49, 101, 108, 113
unmentionables, 100
Urquhart, 22, 212

Vaux, cant lexicographer, 139
Vulliamy, C. F., 105-6

Wallace, Edgar, 73, 76
wallah, 136
Walpole, Horace, 10

wangle, 150, 204
Ware, J. Redding, 139, 146
Warren, S., 66
wassail, 58
Webster, Noah, 108, 113
Weekley, Prof. E., 3, 6, 17, 22, 24, 26, 42, 56-7, 66, 69, 71, 79, 81, 82, 87-9, 91, 97, 98, 108, 112, 119, 135-52 *passim*, 164, 218
Welsh (pejorative), welsher, 8
Welsh rabbit, 8
Wesley, John, 105-12
Whibley, C., 117
Whitney, Wm. D., 113
win, 138, 140, 206, 220
wind up, windy, 203, 213-14
Wiper(s), 148
wood-pecker, 131
work, the art of lightening, 42-52
wounded in slang, 194-5
Wright, Joseph, 27, 28, 47-51 *passim*, 53, 83, 139, 216, 218
Wycherley, 69
Wyld, Prof. H. C., 43, 79, 108, 113, 118

Ya-Ya, 221
yeggs, 76
Yiddish, 28, 181
young Turk, 3-4
Yule, 56-7
Yule and Burnell, 46

Ziph, 40-1